Praise For *In Service to Love*

"As humans are changing and evolving suddenly, unexpectedly, and at a rapid pace, Darlene Green's *In Service to Love* books may be considered essential guides to help people who are ready to accept the guidance of the Council of Light with Darlene working as their scribe. This is an important book. Please order yours today."

"This is a book to add to your collection and perhaps purchase extra copies to share with friends and family. Highly recommended to one and all."

—My Shelf

"*In Service to Love* has a lot to offer during these turbulent times and could provide much-needed comfort, guidance, support, and strength to those who decide to work with the information."

—New Spirit Journal

"This book is a beautiful invitation to discover your full and complete self. We know our physical self. But this series of three books will help us rediscover the amazing beings that we really are. I am eagerly looking forward to reading the next two books!" ★★★★★

—Linda Justice, on NetGalley

"If you are searching for inspirational, feel-good books, then you may want to try out the series *In Service to Love*. Through practice exercises, such as … what happens if you think bigger than you ever have?, these books take readers beyond perceived limitations to a new expanded awareness."

—Lori's Book Loft

"This fascinating daily journal shows us how to balance our lives and energy and appreciate the relationship to the Divine within us. Anyone interested in their energetic connection to the world around them will find this guide to the universe invaluable."

—Caregiver Warrior

IN SERVICE TO LOVE
BOOK 3: LOVE NOW

In Service to Love
Book 3: Love Now

A Dynamic Experience of Consciousness, Transformation, and Enlightenment

DARLENE GREEN
Emissary of Love

Printed in the United States of America

First Printing, 2020

ISBN-13: 978-1-949001-69-3 print edition
ISBN-13: 978-1-949001-70-9 ebook edition

Waterside Productions

Waterside Productions
2055 Oxford Ave
Cardiff, CA 92007
www.waterside.com

To Love.

Dance your dance, Beloved, sing your song;
create on the canvas of your life that which makes your heart soar.

IN SERVICE TO LOVE

A Dynamic Experience of Consciousness, Transformation, and Enlightenment

In Service to Love Book 1: Love Remembered, Days 1–122
In Service to Love Book 2: Love Elevated, Days 123–244
In Service to Love Book 3: Love Now, Days 245–366
Visit the author online at www.darlenegreenauthor.com.

Love's Calling

The conscious journey to enlightenment is not a task to be undertaken; it is a calling. When you find the external world no longer provides the answers you seek, your heart directs you to look where you have not looked before. Your divine nature is present whether you seek it or not. Each step taken in the journey of enlightenment is a threshold to be crossed to your next discovery.

The prerequisites are presence in the moment and a willingness to release what you thought you knew so you may embrace your divine nature. When you connect with your essence, each moment becomes an opportunity to be guided to your best life lived Now. The path of enlightenment is not one with some far-off reward. Your reward is garnered in each moment as you remove the blindfold of illusion and see the truth of the beauty around you, and that IS You.

In the birthing of Love's voice, All rejoice. Hallelujah!

LOVE
December 25, 2019

TABLE OF CONTENTS

BOOK 3: LOVE NOW

Beloved, now that you have released who you are not; now that you have handed over the limited views of your Self to the divine; you see. You see who you have always been. You stand at the open door, the threshold of what now may BE. Guided by your own divine essence, your life is directed by the calling of your soul.

Now is the beginning. Beloved, we have always stood beside you. What Now is possible?

LOVE

WELCOME

As with any journey, arrival at the destination is not the only point. The gifts, beauty, and depth of the experience are available only as each step is taken. This book is the culmination of a process that I don't fully understand, yet one I deeply and sacredly recognize. As I continue to lean into the edge of the unknown, I challenge my human nature and embrace my wholeness. The discoveries are brought into my life as ways of being that bring a broad perspective of peace, connection, compassion, freedom, innovation, beauty, and Love. I continue to feel more like ME.

The writing of *In Service to Love* calls forth all of me. With the presence of divine hands outstretched in guidance daily, I release my deepest sense of limitation to embrace my greatest and most expansive nature. The work of *In Service to Love Book 3: Love Now*, although scribed over two years ago, continues to reveal its wisdom. As I edit the work, I experience the high frequency messages, light infusions, and meditations and am gifted again, as I am met where I am Now. And so it is with multidimensional work.

The uniqueness of this work resides in the divine hands held out in invitation not only to me but to you, gently urging us to see beyond the limitations of our human nature to claim our divine essence as a reality to be lived. Every step, every concept, is lovingly offered for consideration. This work is the bridge from living as a human being having a spiritual experience to living the reality of a spiritual being having a human experience. In our BE-coming, we claim our wholeness and live from the balance of our human nature and divine nature in the way that answers our soul's call.

In Service to Love Book 3: Love Now, is the culmination of all the work, offering guidance, light, and frequency that shines upon possibilities that are ours to discover. The doors are open to thriving on all levels as we choose to cross the threshold of the new global paradigm, claiming our wholeness, full potency and vision.

When the touchstones of your physical world shift,
your divine, inner North Star is ever present.

A New Global Reality

We were all hoping life would remain the same, somewhat reliable, something we could count on so we could focus on other things. All the while we have been feeling the groundswell of a new paradigm for years and decades. When the pressure of the tectonic plates of the earth's crust reaches its maximum, and something has to give, we have an earthquake. In the same way, the feeling we have been sensing is a shift so dramatic and far-reaching, life will never be the same. We are in that Now moment. A pivot in life that will come to define life as we know it; a marker for what life was before and life will be after a global pandemic.

The current global experience is one that joins humanity, allowing us to see how intricately we are connected. Our most potent choice is how to BE within these circumstances. The natural tendency would be arguing for the restoration of what has been, so we may settle into the comfort of knowing our world. Consider that "what has been" is no longer available. We cannot un-live this time, or deny our global responsibility. Living in the space of "Now what?" is a potent stance that acknowledges presence in the moment and openness to possibility.

I have tremendous faith in humanity. I have an unwavering faith in God/Source/Love. Consider the possibility that the journey you have undertaken over the last many years, whether you have been conscious of it or not, has placed you in the perfect spot for Now.

Consider you have all you need. Consider that you are enough. Consider that WE are enough. I see the divine timing of this work guiding us into a new paradigm that holds the full light of our truth, wholeness, and unity.

WE have the say on which perspective we choose. I choose the perspective that invites the best of me to show up so I may BE Love Now. I honor you in your sacred journey of discovery and the exquisite expression of your soul's voice. Thank you for holding the courage and tenacity that it takes to move beyond the perception of limitation. You are a leader in the turning of this evolutionary tide. You have answered Love's call. This is just the beginning.

> In Service to Love,
> Darlene Green
> March 2020
> Seattle, Washington

A Message from the Council of Light

You are invited to engage with your own divine process.
The invitation rests upon the altar of your sacred space.
As you choose a new perspective, to see what's possible, to see what
you have not seen before, we are here. Love beckons. When you
choose to accept the invitation upon your altar, we begin.

In Service to Love addresses an imbalance in life experience. The collective consciousness that is pervasive is one that represents old ways of being. Much of the pain within the physical experience reflects the separation that exists in consciousness between who you are, your perceptions, and how you live. You are on the precipice of a new world, one that is in alignment with who you are as a divine expression of God.

The purpose of our divine collaboration is to offer a new way of being that is in alignment with your innate divine expression and allows you to be in the physical experience in a way that is seamless. It means that you access all of you, beyond limitations, and live a life that is heart centered and soul centered. From the stance of your divine nature, you hold the light and Love that is you and bring your gifts and light to the world to be the unique expression of Love that you are.

The consciousness that drives many of the world's most visible imbalances at this time is grounded in division and separation. This applies to all areas of concern; the environment, politics, and humanitarian crises. In order to transform these issues, you are invited to move to a place where your best resides. Your best resides beyond your perceived limitations and the consciousness of past eras, in a new space that is inhabited only in the Now moment, where you have available the vision to create from your highest expression. You are already the answer. When you align with your highest expression, your frequency is naturally at a level that is authentic for you, you hold the light of Love, and your presence transforms. When you align with your divine truth, you hold space for collaboration of the highest form, which brings heaven to earth and opens new avenues of possibility and ways of being. You hold open the space of possibility that is divinely created. When you align with the limited frequency and consciousness that is the reflection of the problem, there can be nothing else possible beyond more of the same. As you choose the "more" that resides beyond what you already know, you access the vast expanse of your being and the light of possibility. The vibrating field of potential that is guided by the sacredness of being is catalyzed.

What can be possible as you align with your divine nature? Equally, what is no longer possible within the framework and pervasive presence of Love?

The challenge is to BE the courage that is willing to see beyond what is taken for granted, and then, through your inspired moments, to move into action and BE all that is for you to BE.

YOU are the light of the world. Now what?

Love Now Within a New Paradigm

As you allow the restricting view of fear to fall around you like the spring blossoms that give way to summer's leaves, what is revealed is your authentic Self. Beyond the judgment, expectations, and managing of your life is YOU. Beyond circumstance, you, as your essential Self, is not diminished. You, as your authentic Self are the beauty of human nature informed by your divine nature. As your human nature is entwined with your divine essence, you bring to your life the wisdom, clarity, peace, compassion, and the grace that is only you. Informed by your I AM Self in the Now moment, with the limitations of fear released, you soar. You walk in the light of the divine and you live your moments guided by the sacred.

Beloved, look in the mirror, see your divine nature. It is time for you to BE all that you came here to BE. In living a life that is worthy of you, there will be difficulty to overcome. This is an open door; an invitation, for you to show up in your life fully. Who you are is beauty, compassion, innovation, joy, connection, wisdom, friendship, teacher, healer, visionary, believer, and more. You have already walked the difficult path of not being who you are authentically. Showing up now, as who you are requires less effort than hiding your brilliance. All you must do is BE. Be fully present in the Now moment, align with your divine essence, and remember how to listen from the depths of silence.

The Council of Light
March 2020
Seattle, Washington

About the Author

An innate empath, teacher, and healer, Darlene was aware of her Council as early as four years of age. Profound events and sensitivities revealed an ability to reach beyond the reality seen by most. Darlene found a home for her sensitivities as she began studying vibrational healing in 1992. She has written and led programs on living consciously, beginning in 1998 in Seattle, Washington. As a practitioner of Natural Force Healing and a Reiki master, she has utilized her intuitive gifts as a massage therapist practicing in clinical settings in Seattle from 1992 to 2012, when she left to answer a deeper calling. At sacred sites in Southern France, Darlene connected powerfully with her Council of Light and returned to her ancient heritage as Scribe. In 2015 Darlene was invited to create and host a radio program in Phoenix, Arizona, through VoiceAmerica's 7th Wave Channel, titled *The Inner Frontier*, the first step into a global reach. All external work ended as of a severe auto accident early in 2017 when focus turned deeply inward for healing.

On December 26, 2017, Darlene awoke to exalted spiritual events and an invitation by the Council of Light for divine collaboration in a body of work titled *In Service to Love*.

Darlene resides in Seattle with her husband, Ed Green, and their sweet golden retriever, Hailey Grace.

About the Council of Light

Composed of Masters, the Council of Light includes the voices of: Jesus, Mary Magdalene, Archangel Michael, Archangel Gabriel,

Melchizadek, Infinite Oneness, Isis, the Elohim, Buddha, Sanat Kumara, Metatron, the Hathors, Gaia, the Grandmothers, the Grandfathers, St. Germain, Legions of Light, and many more. The Council's presence is vast. The configuration shifts depending on the topic. Thoth, as "Patron of the Scribe" is the facilitator of frequency in light. The experience of the Council of Light is one of Love itself. Throughout the year of writing *In Service to Love*, the Council of Light evolves, from identification of individual Masters to the singular voice of Love.

APPRECIATION

To God, to Source, to Love, thank you for taking my hand and leading me on the divine journey of *In Service to Love*. And there is more as I continue to fine-tune my sensing and balance living within the exquisite beauty of the physical world and hearing the exalted voices of Masters. To all members of the Council of Light, indistinguishable from Love, I thank you for your loving, generous guidance, and ongoing invitation to live up to my I AM, beyond the boundaries of perception. Daily I see your outstretched hand inviting me to step into my wholeness.

Thank you to my family. Thank you, Debbie and Bonnie for your Love and support as over the years you have been a safe place for me to share the gifts I did not yet comprehend. You are cherished beyond measure. My Love and appreciation for you is boundless. I know as we move forward together, led by Love, we honor those of our family that have come before us, the family yet to be and the greater family of humanity. With each step I take, I see the perfection of this journey as it continues to reveal new vistas. Thank you, Shelley, Mark B., Rob H., Mark S., Sean, Brandon, Cara, Bailey, and Parker for being beautiful gifts in my life. The blessing of your presence has formed the canvas of living upon which I create. You are held always in Love, appreciation, and grace.

Kenny and Michelle, you have filled my heart with the joy, sweetness, and generosity of your presence. As you move into new stages of your lives with your families may you be blessed with living from your heart's voice. Thank you, Deb, Hannah, Colby, Braedon, and

Mason for the gift of you. May your footsteps upon the earth be in answer to your own soul's calling. You are beautiful, "like a rainbow."

I have been blessed to have met Masters in form who in profound moments contributed greatly to the expansion of my awareness. Thank you, Esther Hicks, Maureen St. Germain, Sheila and Marcus Gillette. Danielle Rama Hoffman, our meeting was destined. I thank you all for supporting the ignition of my own divine remembering through the sacred alchemy of your presence.

KahMaRea M., I am inspired and gifted by our sisterhood. Your implicit trust in the power of Love has guided your mission this lifetime. You are truly In Service to Love. I will never forget the joy of our five-hour lunches. Just the best.

Thank you to my sisterhood circle. I am delighted and blessed by our journey together. Thank you, Lynn H., and Kristin W., for walking the path of transformation with me over the years. Thank you, Bethany F., and MaSanda G., for your Love and contribution, not only to me; I celebrate the gift you are for the world. Thank you, Mary M., Terri G., SandraAlyse W., Laima Z., Mary A., and Jeff S. We have fulfilled the vow of connecting at this most pivotal time of transformation. What a beautiful alliance of divine light.

I have been guided by synchronicity to Bill Gladstone of Waterside Productions Inc. Thank you for saying yes to *In Service to Love*. Thank you to all in the Waterside Productions family for your guidance and support. Frank Ferrante, I am gifted by the magic of our meeting. Thank you for your contribution to transformation. Thank you, Randall Libero, Senior Executive Producer of VoiceAmerica Talk Radio and TV, for your kindness and patience as I realized a global reach. Thank you, Fauzia Burke, John Burke, and Anna Sacca, of FSB Associates, for holding the expansive vision of *In Service to Love*.

Thank you, Jeanne Kreider, and Dave Kreider of Bellevue Wellness Center, and Kenneth Y. Davis, DC, and Lisa Davis of davisahs.com, for your healing support, vision, and teaching. Your vision those many years ago has lighted the path for the realization of my destiny.

Thank you, Heather Clarke, Founder of Arizona Enlightenment Center, for holding the vision of enlightenment. Thank you, Maria Radloff, for your support and guidance. You are still the best. Thank you, Joanne, of Joanne West Photography, for your vision and brilliant light. My heart smiles.

So many people have contributed to me that it is impossible to name each person with the acknowledgment that fully recognizes the gift you are to me. I send Love and appreciation to each of you unnamed here but indelibly present in my heart. Thank you.

Thank you, Ed G., Debbie B., Bonnie H., KahMaRea M., Kristin W., Katannya C., Michelle W., Mary M., Terri G., Mary A., Jeff S., Lynn H., Sheryl T., Heather C., Lynn L., Tresje S., Marcia P., and Mary R., for graciously receiving the daily words of *In Service to Love*.

Ed, I choose you. Thank you for walking this beautiful path with me. I recognized you when we met. The tapestry of our lives is woven with the fulfillment of Love's promise. I hold you gently in the golden light of Love and appreciation.

In Love always,
Darlene

Walking Enlightenment

Walking enlightenment is not always a path of unicorns and dough-nuts. Walking the path of enlightenment means you bring all of you to each moment in your life. It means you have taken responsibility for being your Self in your wholeness as you are able to express it in the moment. Enlightenment is not a separation from living in the physical realm. Enlightenment allows you to experience your Self and your life from an expansive perspective. You will notice that you will feel the pain of those around you more. You will notice you will feel the pain of the earth more. You will feel the action or inaction of the collective consciousness more acutely as well. You see and you will know more, because your senses have been tuned to the fine frequencies of your own soul. And so, you sense acutely from your multidimensionality. What you also hold is divine perspective, previously unavailable. You have the ability to choose your frequency. You may shift your frequency by choice. When you are feeling weighed down by events of the world or of your life, remember your ability to access perspective, where what was hidden is revealed, allowing clarity.

As you continue to live on the edge of the known and unknown realms, because there is never any end to your evolutionary movement, you will notice the edge of the known and unknown follows you like a shadow. The fears you held for staying small may not vanish completely in the brilliant light of your divine truth. Allow, dear One, the fears to walk beside you as you continue to choose the path of your own divine essence. You will experience the discomfort of an edge that at times compels you to your next step. When you experience the exalted and exquisite beauty of your own divine connection it is at times startling to also be reminded of the density of humanity. Now, *as an enlightened being, having connected with your own essential Self, you own the gradient of light expression that is you. Dwelling in the chaos of your internal fears is now an indulgence to the lower-frequency part of you. You have the ability to rise like the phoenix to the heights of your divine essence. You see the challenges in front of you as an opportunity for something yet to be revealed. As you hold the space of choosing clarity, choosing to BE Love, choosing to express your greatest you, you know you will move beyond difficulties. You walk with ease at the edge of the known and unknown realms.*

You have the ability to hold a powerful and potent perspective. That is your gift. You hold the door open for possibility. You hold the vision for alignment that brings peace, grace, and Love for All. And you honor the choice of those that have chosen something else. Your perspective is great enough you see that All truly is well. You see the perfection in each moment and grasp the opportunity to BE your perfect expression of Love Now. You respond to life, inspired by your highest expression, and bring your best into the world living the contribution you came here to be. As you take responsibility for being your greatest Self, the barriers that once stopped you vanish in your intention. You no longer blend in. You stand out to be seen and heard, and to contribute.

You now know you are the answer. You ARE the light of the world. You hold infinity in your hand and the emanations of the divine within your heart. Your greatest work is you being you.

The Council of Light

DAY 245: HALLS OF LIGHT

The process of expanding awareness is an ever-moving landscape. As you choose to access more of the light expression that is authentically you, your perspective shifts, altering your relationship to the physical world. Enlightenment is a process that must alter your reality. The shift reflects the access to more of your awareness that resides in the realms of light as your I AM Self. As you express from your divine essence, you bridge worlds. Your reality is experienced as multidimensional, reflecting your true nature. Your awareness in light accelerates, extending beyond the reach of your thought. Our collaboration supports your awareness and the integration of your movement in light with ease and grace. More natural to you than breathing, the experience of enlightenment is wholeness, and of being home. Enlightenment is you, being All of you.

Increasingly you will find frequency as background to the words you read. Today's conversation is one where rich frequency support is available. There are pivotal moments in your expansion of consciousness as your awareness is no longer linear. Multidimensional expression is met with multidimensional conversation and process. If you so choose, we guide you into the space prepared by Masters, who pave your way. The Halls of Light is an environment that addresses your unique process, working differently with each person who chooses this respite. A place of wholeness, Love, light, and unity, initiation into the Halls of Light acts as a catalyst for your next perfect step. We will move forward if you choose it to be so.

Initiation into the Halls of Light

If you are a "yes" for this initiation, we commence. Sit down or lie down and be comfortable. Watch the movement of your breath. Allow your awareness to move to stillness. Feel the presence of the Masters in attendance. You are held in the divine light of a crystalline chapel. Each crystalline form around you reverberates in Love. You are bathed in the expansive expression of Love, grace, and peace. As you relax into the Now moment, you are present with your I AM Self. Your divine expression informs you through light, and perhaps with words. Allow your senses to expand, matching the high frequency experience of the moment. You will notice a sensation of fluidity as your awareness expands.

When you feel complete, restored, and refreshed, bring your attention back to the physical surroundings holding the gift of light in your knowing.

You have been here many times, often with Masters who are present here today. The process of enlightenment brings your divine nature to conscious awareness. When you hear the notes of your soul, added to by the harmonies of Love, the true nature of you gifts your Now moments.

It is in Love, with Love, from Love that we remain,

In Service to Love

DAY 246: THE TRANSCENDENT QUALITY OF ALIGNMENT

We speak ongoingly about the aligning of you in your human nature with your divine nature. There are many ways to embrace your wholeness. We emphasize conscious alignment with your essential Self for many reasons. It is within the alignment of your human nature with your I AM Self that you may live your physical life from a perspective that is transcendent. The alignment of your divinity and humanity allows you to live beyond perceived barriers to experience your greatest life now. As you continue to gain a broader perspective, your relationship to experiences in your day-to-day living shifts. Those that are present in light today hold open the experience for you to recognize your divine essence. We as Masters are not to be emulated. We are teachers, reminding you of the divine expression that IS you. Those present today greet you eye to eye, divine to divine, and peer to peer; Jeshua, Melchizadek, Infinite Oneness, Legions of Light, Archangel Michael, the White Brotherhood, Buddha, Metatron, Mary Magdalene, Isis.

When you step back to hold a vast perspective, you see broader elements of creation. You begin to see how your being, frequency, and intentions cast more weight in the creative process than the list of to-do items that seem logical from your human perspective. As you hold the space open for alignment with your highest expression, your essential Self may then take the wheel.

When you see that your divine expression is at the control of your day, the usual methods of doing seem less fruitful. Not that action isn't helpful, but in the process of alignment with your I AM presence, action is directed from the inner realms first, through inspiration, clarity, impulse, and resonance.

When you see, really see, that who you are is Source in form, you no longer play small. When you realize your divine access, it is *You* that you look to for clarity. The veil of illusion is not a mandatory experience. At this time in the evolutionary process, the door is open for your discovery of and communion with your I AM Self. It's not something that is important to most; however, you wouldn't be reading these words if it weren't important to you. In answer to your calling, we are *In Service to Love.* Our greatest message is not of our history, or our footsteps while incarnated; our message to you is to remind you of your divine essence, your sacred heritage, available as the baptismal font to anoint a new reality.

When you connect with your wholeness you must see your Self as more than human. You are a being of light extending into form. As a hand fits into a glove, your physical expression is the glove. The greatest part of you, beyond the glove, resides in light. It is the light that controls the physical. As you connect with your divine expression that resides in light, you see newly.

These principles are demonstrated to your Scribe during her day. The realization is that the micromanaging of her day need not occur. She feels and trusts that all truly is well. She feels guidance through her day from her highest Self. She is placed at the right place at the right time. All this is experienced with the greatest expression of joy, peace, Love, and freedom.

We ask you to consider how, during your day's moments, your I AM is at the helm. When your I AM Self is at the helm of your life, you see where you have gotten out of your own way to experience your truth. You see that the restrictions and perceived limitations of physical expression no longer hold weight.

This is the journey of enlightenment.

DAY 247: WALK WITH ME

What is it, dear One, that you would want to hear? What is it that troubles you? It is in moments of your need and discontent that we answer. We are available in each moment, sharing your discoveries and joy and your concerns and worry. It is not as though the solution to everything is your joy. The art of living lies within the ability to navigate all aspects of being, including the troubling moments. Hiding how you feel is not the answer. Walk with me. Walk with this divine Council of Light. We are here beside you. Moving to the forefront within this divine Council of Light this afternoon is Jeshua, Buddha, Archangel Gabriel, Archangel Michael, the White Brotherhood, Mary Magdalene, Melchizadek, and Isis.

Who you are in your divine expression embraces every facet of your being; the parts of you that feel accomplished, the parts of you that you see as lacking; all is embraced in the space of Love. There is value in giving those parts of you that hold discomfort or hold worry a voice. As you allow the energy to move through those parts of you that feel fear, judgment, worry, that feel less than, you allow those parts of your being space to evolve. As the space for evolution is created, those parts of you that feel not as evolved or fulfilled may be informed by your highest knowing. As you hold tight or push away the parts of you that feel restricted, there is no opportunity for their transformation. Then as you continue to expand in conscious awareness, it is as though the parts of being that request attention receive no oxygen and the chasm within you grows and deepens.

Trust the transcendent quality of your alignment. Seek the highest counsel available. Allow space for Love's transformation.

Walk with us, reveal those parts of you that feel less than, so that they may feel the warmth of Love's embrace. Allow them to move and evolve. Unity consciousness requests bringing all parts of you into wholeness. Who you are is Source in form. You do the greatest service to all parts of your being as you allow them to be exposed to the truth of your authentic nature. The parts of you that feel restricted are present at this time to be allowed into Love's light.

From the perspective of your totality, the parts of you that seek light will show up for healing as your conscious awareness expands. Even parts of you that you thought had already healed may surface, requesting a new perspective. When that occurs, acknowledge the part of you that holds fear and walk hand-in-hand in Love. Allow the concern to be communicated. Then from your I AM Self, welcome home all parts of your being. Understand that your truth never changes.

As you align with your divine nature, the resonance of your truth will reverberate throughout your whole being. Areas of concern that seek Love's light will come to your awareness. You may also be feeling the pain of the earth's changes. Remember to step back in your perspective to the point you see where all truly is well. As you BE the expression of Love that is your authentic nature, you bring healing.

You are never alone. We walk with you. Talk with us, get to know us Now.

DAY 248: CONSENSUS AND RESONANCE

It is human nature to need the understanding of those around you. Though you look for ways to comprehend your expanding awareness, your divine nature resides beyond the limits of human nature. The experience is much like learning a new language that holds familiarity and with which you are not yet fluent.

As your process of expanding awareness accelerates in velocity, your new language becomes one of the subtleties of resonance. Consensus, which is the agreement that supports choices you have already made, becomes moot. Consensus is external agreement. The only purpose consensus serves now is for the personality. At times, your Scribe also has difficulty in believing this is actually occurring, that she is conferring with Masters. She finds she looks for consensus in her experience. As she, and you, move along the gradient scale of light expression, consensus is something that holds you back and provides a distraction from listening to and honing skills to fine-tune your inner referencing. We make this distinction to support you in continuing the process of recalibrating your awareness. This becomes a journey of One. It is not a journey of All. It is as you move to the perspective of being the One that you are more able to hear the fine whisperings of your highest knowing, unfiltered through the awareness of personality. The journey from consensus to resonance is the journey of external referencing to internal knowing.

The experience of wanting more people to understand your process becomes an increasing challenge. Collective consciousness is a potent force that holds a group consensus. Now as you align with your divine nature you seek the singular note that is yours. The note that is yours alone is beyond the listening of others. There is often resonance in similar pathways, but you will find your divine essence is unique to you.

The note you listen for is yours alone. Resonance is the beacon that affirms your direction. Look to fine-tune your awareness of resonance. Before you were consciously conscious, you still found yourself moving in a direction that was toward your own inner light. How could that have happened? There are many layers of resonance that have always and will always guide you beyond your understanding of it. There is an element of trust and faith in the divine expression that is you. As you begin to relax and know you've got this, you also engage the mechanisms that are part of your natural repertoire.

One of the most challenging concepts for you to really embrace is the fact of your own divinity. When you embrace the mastery you already hold, you allow the full expression of your divine nature; you give it space to manifest. As you no longer hold barriers to your truth, the fullness of your unique expression is a gift for All.

DAY 249: EMERGENCE

Accessing your divine truth is a lifetime of exploration. Once you begin to realize your truth, you bring into form all that had been residing in light. Realization is one thing, actualization is another. Today we speak of the burst of energy created by the velocity of your expansion that in turn ushers into form the wisdom of your divine nature.

As you reach into the light of you, you begin to touch your divine essence. In the same way the butterfly must emerge from the chrysalis, so it is with you. You will notice at each stage of the enlightenment process that more is revealed. Once you become aware of your true nature (realization) you have the opportunity then to fulfill your highest expression (actualization). In the butterfly analogy, the caterpillar is realizing potential within the chrysalis. When she emerges as a butterfly, potential is actualized. Realization and actualization are the cycle of expansion that transforms your reality.

Understanding which part of the cycle you occupy is valuable as you set your energy accordingly. If you are within the chrysalis phase, energy is not available outwardly. When you are in the actualization phase, energy becomes available for external expression. You will notice there is a burst of energy that becomes available as you are getting ready to emerge from the chrysalis. Do you see that life knows how to live? You have already within your design the energetic sequencing that matches and supports your process of enlightenment. Trust the brilliance of your unique process. You already have all you need.

The design of your highest expression is already positioned for manifestation into form. Relax and trust your own brilliance. There is nothing to do other than follow the wisdom of your resonance. When you are aligned with your I AM Self, you connect with the positioning and alignment available for manifestation. Follow your own flow and you find the ease you may be supported within.

You create daily. Understanding the components of creation is a potent tool for manifesting consciously.

We delight in your discovery of your brilliance.

Day 250: The Brass Ring

It is I, Thoth, stepping to the forefront of this divine conversation within this Now immaculate moment. Bring your awareness to the time before this lifetime; before you chose to incarnate into the life you are now living. That is the inter-life. You conferred, you researched, you came to this physical experience for a purpose. Today, we ask you to focus on your original intention for this life.

In your own perfect divine timing, you chose this lifetime, in this evolutionary period. There was a knowing, a sense of direction, a template of intention that was your plan. With all the details filled in, it is possible to connect with your original intention for this life you live Now. Are you aligned? Do you have a sense of your soul's direction? Is there a feeling of something missing, like a puzzle piece that would complete the picture? Your plan calls upon access to your divine nature, light, and wisdom. Your original intention waits for you to arrive at clarity.

With the same comfort you have in your physical world, meeting the intention of your soul is within your grasp. As you navigate your light awareness, look for the signposts of your original intention. Look deeper. As you look for your original mandate, you will find qualities that challenge your limited view of Self. Look for the expression that is worthy of you, not what you deem possible.

We bring a question to you this evening. What is your original mandate? As you place the inquiry into a space of examination, you ignite the parts of you that hold clarity.

Consider employing the aspect of you that is the explorer, traversing vast spaces previously uncharted. What is the next expression that is calling you into action?

The contemplation of your original mandate is the question which, when placed in inquiry, invites answers. Where you focus attention, you gain awareness. The brass ring is within reach.

Day 251: Naturally

You are the architect of your life, with many tools at your disposal. The tool we speak of in the instance of expanding consciousness is your divine nature. It is easy to think of yourself as a mere mortal. That is a paradigm that has held you ensconced in the illusion of separation.

After you read each day's contribution of *In Service to Love*, there is a natural pull to go back to the normalcy of your day. We encourage you to begin a new tack. BE with the truth, resonance, and frequency of the words, beyond your thinking or beliefs about them; understand that you have beliefs and thoughts that hold you in bondage. This body of work is not something new to encase within limitation. Human nature seeks sameness and comfort, mostly occurring below your awareness. Moving unconscious perception to the surface of conscious awareness is critical in the process of enlightenment. Consider that how you do your enlightenment process is how you do everything. Conversely, as you move through your process of expanding awareness, there are opportunities for new perspectives everywhere. We suggest that living with resistance is hard work. You will notice a beautiful flow in your life as you release limitation and engage your own divine nature. Being who you are, fully actualized, is the You that you strive for as your most natural expression.

The Hamster Wheel of Beliefs

There are limitations hidden within belief systems. The main point being, if you have made decisions about who you are, then all other possibilities are off the table. There is no possibility available to experience anything beyond your beliefs. Consider that the same holds true for the beliefs of cultures and collective consciousness itself.

Beliefs live as an eternal hamster wheel. Beliefs held unconsciously look something like:

- *You hold a set of beliefs.*
- *Choices are made in life that fit within the boundaries of beliefs.*
- *The result is life within the beliefs you have set.*
- *The "proof" continues to show up in your reality, proving you are right.*
- *Your beliefs are reinforced, building the wall between you and possibility.*

Unconscious expression is a part of human nature. However, we recommend a new perspective of consciousness. When you allow your choices to be informed by internal referencing, beyond your beliefs, you are connected to possibility. Then you continue to have proof of your divine nature expressing itself. When you access your I AM Self to inform your choices, you allow space for your wholeness to be lived.

Beliefs held consciously are the door to your freedom. Beliefs then turn to choices. When you can choose consciously, you create from the perspective of your divine mastery. Held below the level of your consciousness, beliefs live in opposition to your expansion. Hold the intention for the unseen to be seen. Allow the next barrier to your expanding consciousness to rise into your awareness.

We place on the altar this evening the consideration of leaving your beliefs at the door before you sit down to read *In Service to Love.* Then allow time after reading to hold the door open, so to speak.

Just this experience of holding your default system of beliefs at bay will result in a release of the baggage that holds you down, with new choices and possibilities arising in your awareness.

We, as Master teachers, stand before you under the shade of the ancient olive trees, as we have many times before. We remind you of your own divine destiny, fulfilled by no one other than you. Your uniqueness is being called forth. What becomes possible?

Day 252: Pure Essence

From the moment you said yes to *In Service to Love*, we have been in collaboration. It is the pure essence of you that said, "Yes." It is the pure essence of your being that moves you consciously along the path of enlightenment to the realization of all that you are.

As we refer to your essential being, we point to the you at your most authentic Self: Source extended into form where your human nature and divine nature are perfectly integrated. Your wholeness is an experience beyond imagining to your most joyous, most connected, most fulfilled, free, creative, potent expression. The intention of our conversation today is to shine light upon the goal of this collaboration. As you begin to consider possibility, you open the space for clarity. To find out who you are, at your pure essence, be with us as you consider suspending who you think you are at this moment—and imagine.

Experience Your Essential State

Be still. Relax into your breath. Raise your frequency gently, feeling the weight, the concerns of your mind fall away easily. Notice the feeling of expansive awareness. From the space of noticing, sense your most potent Self. Find your space of stillness. Temporarily place upon the altar those things that limit the view of your divine reality. This is the act of temporarily suspending your thoughts and beliefs. And then you may find new possibilities.

From the open space before you, feel the absence of boundaries. Feel the absence of thought. Beyond thought, beyond belief, exists the state of being from the perspective of your totality. From this space we ask you to again suspend what you know. Allow the light expression of you beyond form to come to your awareness. Feel the presence of the sacred, feel the space of Love that is pervasive. Yet unnamed, your potential awaits direction in order to catalyze creation. Be in this space as you are guided.

Within the space of no thought, within the perfection of the Now immaculate moment, is your vast, pure essence.

When you are complete, return to your physicality feeling connected, balanced, rested, and re-sourced by Love.

Release

When you sit to meditate or create your intentions for the day, a most powerful action is asking to place what does not serve you upon the sacred space of your altar. It is one way to release beliefs, thoughts and judgments, allowing your pure essential state to be accessed consciously.

The experience of your pure essential Self is potent. An alchemical experience, you will notice your reality shifting into alignment. As you Be with no thought, you support the aligning of your highest expression with your conscious awareness. You will feel the vast space you occupy. You may sense fluidity. You will feel your natural state of Love. Practice aligning with your divine nature.

The experience of one's pure essence is beyond thought. It is beyond words, encompassing All. Pure essence does not react. Pure essence creates from the impulse of Source. Pure essence is the space of knowing, of directing, of experiencing All, informing the physical, yet not limited by the details of form.

When we speak of releasing the you that you think you know, we speak of then allowing your truth, your divine nature, space to consciously navigate. The result is clarity, and the sacred connection to All. The result is the experience of Love, and the impulse is one of living your soul's vision.

DAY 253: A DROP IN THE OCEAN

As you place one foot in front of the other on the pathway to enlightenment, there is a point where you must align yourself with more clarity as Source. We have avoided the more charged words and concepts like God, Creator, because they are laden with limitations as defined by collective consciousness. We refer to you as Source in form, and today we bring more light to that concept. Within your unique expression is a vast knowing and connection with All that is. Again, available only from a distant perspective, we ask you to loosen yourself from the bonds of your beliefs yet again, and step back farther, back to your I AM Self. Those present in light tonight beckon you forth to see newly from perhaps the broadest perspective you have experienced while in form. Stepping to the forefront and joining with their voices are Jeshua, Mary Magdalene, Isis, Infinite Oneness, Archangel Michael, Sanat Kumara, Melchizadek, Metatron, and Legions of Light.

As we have journeyed so far within *In Service to Love*, we have traversed tremendous space, revealing new shores of reality previously unseen, yet recognized by your inner knowing. *In Service to Love* is a magic carpet ride, providing the light that illuminates your arrival at the new, yet familiar, ports of awareness. You will notice concepts have been building in perspective and frequency as the strength of your signature energy has been amplified.

When we say you are Source in form, what does that mean to you? From the perspective of anything other than the experience of your I AM, it is a difficult leap to make. So, we invite you to move to the space of your I AM Self. We have been speaking of this over the past number of days. Within the experience of I AM, there is no thought, yet awareness of All. It is an impeccable experience of being in the immaculate Now moment. Therein is the presence of no-thing and everything. Your I AM Self resides at the point of creation, awaiting the alchemy that catalyzes potential into form. There is no "because" here. There is no "reasoning" here. There is no good, no bad, no past, no future. There is only that which is in alignment with your unique expression as Source, Now.

Source holds infinite expressions. How would you relate one drop of ocean water to the ocean itself? Are they not each of the same stuff? Perhaps some water resides in the warmth of equatorial space, some other drops of water splash above the surf at polar zones. One drop of water holds the awareness of "all ocean," yet experiences itself as warm, cold, frozen, as condensation, or rising as clouds. Consider that the same relationship resides between the expression of Source that you are and All. This concept is foundational to your realization and the ultimate actualization of your highest expression in form.

Understand that this is not a journey undertaken by most. Why would someone want to be in form, yet yearn to learn of that part of them which is not in form? Your pure essence has chosen conscious contribution within this lifetime. From your highest, most vast vantage point there is an inner knowing that seeks expression. You are no longer willing to get to the end of this lifetime in form and, at the last moments, realize your mission was not complete. You chose to be awakened fully at this time in evolution to contribute your divine design in your most perfect, unique, and sacred expression. At this point of evolution, the veil of separation is thin.

The purpose of our collaboration is to support your awakening to your greatest expression. The bells toll for your awakening, realization, and actualization. The path of the Master is not popular. For those who risk greatly, the reward is greater. The Love that you

Be seeks voice. Your alignment with your I AM Self connects you with the Love, peace, freedom, joy, abundance, and more that is inherently yours, available Now.

You see, you, too, are In Service to Love.

DAY 254: LIVING IN PEACE

Good afternoon, dearest Beloveds. It is I, Thoth, stepping to the forefront of this divine conversation within this Now immaculate moment. It is when you choose to live life from the most aligned, natural expression that you find the peace that is also a hallmark of your I AM presence. It is easy to consider peace as conditional. Peace is a principle of being, as is Love. The collective consciousness would state that peace is the absence of conflict and war. We ask you to consider peace as an elevated state of being that supersedes conflict and war. Conflict may not take place within the presence of peace. Those present in light today include Jeshua, Mary Magdalene, Infinite Oneness, Isis, Melchizadek, Metatron, Archangel Michael, and the Council of the Golden Heart.

The absence of peace signifies the presence of limitation and illusion, inherent in the human experience where the veil of separation reigns. One does not have to reside in light to have the experience of peace. There is a saying, when one transitions, "Rest in peace." We ask, "Why not live in peace?" The experience of peace, not as the absence of conflict, but as a potent state of being resides within the Now immaculate moment. There is no history, no limitation, and no beliefs that bring it about. The state of peace is naturally occurring as you are informed by your I AM Self. The more aligned you are with your authentic nature, the greater the experience of peace.

Peace is not a belief to be argued or justified; it is a naturally occurring experience that is more prevalent as you move on the path of expanding conscious awareness. The more of your light you access within your process of enlightenment, actualization, and realization, the greater your experience of peace as an inner way of being.

We would say a few words about that which is not peace, also applicable on a global scale, but we refer more specifically to an individual experience, particularly the inner experience of anxiety. Consider that the collective consciousness within the era of separation consciousness is defined mostly by living not from inner cues and resonance but rather from an external force of beliefs and mores. When you are not aligned with the guiding beacon of your divine nature, anxiety is one resultant experience. It is as though a ship at sea loses its rudder and is then adrift with no direction. The guidance from external sources, such as beliefs, history, and mass consciousness, masquerades as a solution, but it is not an authentic alignment, and the result is an experience of disappointment, frustration, sadness, and anxiety, in the loss of something unidentified. Typically, the experience of anxiety will occur with those individuals who hold a clear mandate for their life, which requires the inner aligning available through the process of enlightenment. Much of anxiety is the experience that says, "You are far away from your own soul's voice. Move closer to Source, move inward, listen to the heartbeat of your own resonance. The answers reside within." Raise the frequency of your thoughts, elevate your awareness beyond the limitations and arguments, and you will begin to find the calm waters of your own divine expression.

If peace is a description of your mandate, become the peace you seek. It happens organically as you more clearly embrace the presence of your I AM Self. Peace becomes part of your emanating structure of light, as does Love. When you take on peace globally, intergalactically, and throughout the multiverse, continue to raise your frequency; move beyond the limitations of form to BE your highest expression. As you follow your internal resonance, you follow the beacon of your own soul's light and you become the peace.

Peace surpasses all understanding. Peace is your authentic nature.

In Love, with Love, from Love,
The Council of Light

Day 255: Waking from the Dream

When you stand back and look from a vast perspective, you see the evolutionary expansion of consciousness that takes place throughout creation. Nothing is still or stopped. All evolves to the next highest expression whether movement is noticed or not. It is this process of evolution that naturally ignites the fire that questions the nature of reality, and that has some people look for the more that their heart seeks. Those present today offer their light of assurance and acknowledgment of your right place within the landscape of expanding conscious awareness and your impact upon all of creation.

The state of unconsciousness is part and parcel of the experience of physical form. Each soul holds the intention of evolving to their next expression. When one is born into the material world within the illusion of separation there burns a deep desire to return home, for wholeness, for the return to Love, and return to Source. The divine nature of each being seeks expression at the highest level. Love must evolve! As the acorn falls from the tree, it holds potential for expressing divine design of the highest level. The design held within the acorn holds the potential for a vital tree that has potential to be centuries old, having weathered the onslaught of challenging circumstances and the ease of perfect conditions. As the tree does not choose circumstances, you do. You choose the circumstance of your life as you move into form to experience your Self.

When you believe that all you see is the extent of reality, the purpose for your expression is the mastery of living behind the veil of illusion. Navigating life in the absence of your divine knowing is the challenge that contributes to your personal evolutionary story. When the questioning extends into the realms beyond the physical, the opening for enlightenment begins and you begin to awaken from the dream of illusion. As you question that which is in front of you, you begin to see behind the curtain of collective consciousness, into a reality that holds the vision of your authentic nature.

As you continue to ask the questions, the opportunity for seeing beyond the walls of perceived limitation opens. At choice in every moment, your reality expands in scope, depth, and dimension. The amount of light you hold is exponentially increased, adding to the light of creation, which in turn acts as a catalyst for more Love to express.

We cannot emphasize enough the impact you have on the presence of Love upon planet Earth and beyond. At the leading edge of evolutionary expression, you hold the light of truth. Your courage to see beyond most buoys the remembering for All.

Day 256: Elevated Awareness

The path of enlightenment is not walked by most. Therefore, it follows that you see beyond the boundaries that contain the collective consciousness. No longer dependent upon physical information alone, you reach your divine nature residing in light through resonance. Your elevated awareness brings a broader range of your expression into play consciously.

As you live from your divine nature, your frequency naturally elevates. Your view of reality resides beyond limitations of the physical realm. And that it is! As you access more information that is contained not only in the *things* around you but in the *air*, you perceive a high level of information that previously had been undetected. Today we speak of the information you process as a part of your expanded awareness.

Picture the analogy of the gradient scale of light that comprises your totality. The gradient demonstrates how you are only partially expressed in the physical realm and more expansively expressed in the realm of light. Enlightenment is a process that draws upon the part of you that resides in light, naturally integrating with the experience of being human, allowing vision beyond limitations. As your awareness expands, you naturally interpret information that is not physical. The set of rules assigned to physical expression hold a limited perspective. As you consider the release of perceived limitations, you will find you access the

possibility that resides within your light expression. As you continue to align with your essential Self, you are informed more
by your expansive field of light and less by the bonds of physical
form.

As you define yourself as being only one facet of expression,
you limit possibility, with no avenue to access what you do not
know. Your nonlinear expression may only be accessed as you
release the hard-and-fast definitions of yourself to allow your
greatest knowing space to land. Does that make sense? As far
as you have moved in your conscious awareness there is always
more. Of that you may be assured. Rely on the magnitude of
possibility that lies within the Now immaculate moment. As you
align with your highest frequency available in the moment, you
access your greatest possibility, which moves your potential into
realization.

Living from an elevated awareness relies upon utilizing the
new rules that accompany high frequency expression. Consider
that assigning at least equal weight to information that comes
to you through resonance, inspiration, clairaudience, clairvoy-
ance, and clairsentience. These are natural tools you have always
had that gather information from the space of high frequency.
Consider, in every question you have, to intend access to your
highest knowing. This will require you to develop an adeptness at
shifting your frequency by choice and looking beyond the realm
you already know.

Earlier we spoke of learning to dance the ladder of frequency.
In this concept you acknowledge the expanse of your awareness
and take ownership of the potency of choice and presence in
the moment. The baggage of the past or the hopes of the future
may not enter. You may move into the Now moment untethered
and then declare intention in the moment that, as you are in the
moment, has room to play out in your life experience. A potent
expression.

Do you see how All resides within you whether you are in form or in light? We hold space for discovery of your perfect design. You are one of a kind. No one may smile and light the universe like you.

Brilliant.

Day 257: Love as Your New Default

With the experience of Love as your default, there is nothing that may stop you. Love, as your way of being, is experienced as waves of bliss, exaltation, deep appreciation, and moments of beauty beyond description. As your Scribe states, "I'm in Love with Love." As you spend more of your day in alignment with your highest expression, you reside increasingly within the high frequency state of Love. From this way of being, the concerns or limitations of physical form lessen as you are informed by your essential Self. Your experience in the moment is a potent creative matrix that accesses your divine design as both a manifestation and clarity of connection in light. We, as the Council of Light, contributing to this divine collaboration in the name of Love, acknowledge the courage and intention it takes to move beyond that which seems comfortable within the default of physical limitations to pursue the more that resides within your essential Self as a divine expression of Love. Love is its own reward.

Declarations of Love

As you hold Love as a principal way of being, you access the creative action you own in light. The clarity, wisdom, and potent creative expression is heightened from presence in the moment as Love. From the experience of Love, allow Love to be the reliable background of your day, and then you create from Love. Manifestation from the matrix of Love is potent. This is the next area for your attention.

When you experience those exalted moments of being Love, declare and create: then receive with Love, grace and appreciation.

> *I declare that what is in alignment with my divine design will manifest in form.*
> *I choose for the abundance and all that is mine, in the name of Love, to manifest.*
> *I choose to be all that is mine to be, as my highest expression, in the name of Love.*
> *I choose to do all that is mine to do, in the name of Love.*
> *I create with purpose, ease, and grace that which is sourced from my I AM Self.*
> *I receive all that is mine to be, do, and have with Love and delight.*

The experience of Love is intoxicating. The beauty is breathtaking. The truth of the moment is indescribable and undeniable. When you experience your Self as Love, you are aligned with your divine essence. At first, the beauty is such a departure from normal that it stops you in your tracks. That is because any lower frequency endeavor is no longer a match in that moment. The experience of Love is possible as a way of being. Love, as experienced in the moment, becomes the new backdrop of your day, perpetually new, as you are sourced from your highest expression in each Now moment. It's like being plugged in to a new power source; a good description of what is occurring energetically.

Understand that when you are in high frequency ways of being, you may create with clarity, purpose and ease that which is in alignment with your highest expression. Continue to feel the ecstasy of Love. When you feel ready, you, as Love, may direct light toward what you choose to create. When you create from Love, there is no because. There is no reasoning. Remember the experience of your I AM presence? There is only choice in the moment. Allow the creation to be big enough for you. Allow the creation to match your exquisite nature. The universe does not qualify your choices. Choose your creation. Then let it be. Drop it. Turn attention in the coming moments and days to that which is aligned in resonance with you. Are you ready to choose the whole enchilada?

These are exciting times. We delight in you taking the wheel of your divine expression. This sets the stage for your divine collaboration. What could that be? Hmmm. Convoy of Love.

DAY 258: NOW; A NEW BEGINNING

Living in the present moment is the opportunity to create in your life from a clean slate, unhindered by the past and unburdened by the future. It is only from the present moment that you may live a life untethered by constraints and fully connected to possibility.

We, as the Council of Light, engage you only in the moment. You engage us from a variety of perspectives. Stepping to the forefront of this divine conversation are Jeshua, Mary Magdalene, Infinite Oneness, Isis, Archangel Gabriel, Archangel Michael, and Melchizadek. Whether you are reading this from the perspective of your past or from your future, the truth of our message of Love will resonate. The quality and clarity of the resonance is affected by the state you are in, in the moment. Like a bell that rings crystal clarity, when you are engaging us from the present moment, the potency of our collaboration is immaculate. The result is the realignment of you to your highest expression. When you engage this work, or your life, for that matter, from the point of concerns and memories from the past or fear of the future, the quality of resonance may be likened to a bell being rung underwater. The efficacy of the resonance, although present, feels more distant and somewhat dulled. Do you see how the path to enlightenment is paved by presence in the moment?

When you are unburdened by the past, the future, or fears of the opinions of others, your true brilliance shines. Your potent stance in the moment has you aligned for all that is yours to be, do, and have. The possibility of potential realized lies within the Now moment.

One of the many gifts of being in the moment is the joy that becomes available. Unburdened, you live beyond limitations. Regardless of circumstance, when your choice is to be present in the moment, you bring the full potency of your being to bear. Your joy, fulfillment, wisdom, clarity, and peace become heightened, and you hold the keys to live your greatest expression.

The path of enlightenment offers many gifts. The practice of presence reveals the universe that is available within the Now moment. Every moment is a new beginning.

DAY 259: A STAND FOR YOUR UNIQUE EXPRESSION

Only you may <u>BE</u> you. You are the missing puzzle piece. The contribution to all creation that you hold is immense. Breaking through the perceived barriers of neutrality and invisibility go hand in hand with the process of actualization. Those of us in light this evening stand for your unique divine expression made manifest.

Your genius seeks articulation. Genius is that which is beyond the bounds of normal and results in a uniquely potent expression. Your genius is powered by the direct alignment with your divine nature. What if your I AM Self were given full expression? Consider that your greatest level of authenticity is achieved as your human nature is integrated with the magnitude of your divine nature. What could be possible?

All the powerful contributions of music, art, literature, and invention have been brought forth through the courage to be authentic, as all great works are sourced from a deep well of inspiration. If you look closely, your contribution is one you already sense. The path of enlightenment invites tempering offered through tenacity. As you forge the path beyond that which is thought as normal, you rise to the rarefied experience of your divine nature. Your genius is requesting expression and the opportunity to be the contribution that you know you are.

The courage to move through the mire and density of collective awareness is part of the process. Most people would say they do not have original thought, thinking perhaps that this is only available to philosophers and the fortunate few. Consider that you have full access to original thought Now. Informed by your divine design, in the Now moment, your potential is limitless. Profound works are yours to be expressed. Original thought is something that stands out in form, quality, and resonance. One can feel the frequency of the origin of the creation. As you are on your path of realizing your divine design, you encounter the barriers and illusions of blending in. It is the moving beyond perceived barriers with no loss of power that holds divine inspiration apart from the mundane.

Awaiting is the potential of your divine nature, realized not through just one idea, thought or creation, but as a continual stream taking many forms. What is the creation that awaits your pen, brush, or a gentle plucking of the strings?

We urge you on, in the realization of your divine expression. The genius you have to offer is not available anywhere else, from anyone else, in the cosmos. Have at it! Relish every delicious discovery.

Day 260: Listening Beyond Your Personality

Our presence today supports you in your efforts to move beyond the limits of perceived barriers. As you expand your conscious awareness at the edge of your inner frontier you experience the resistant push and pull of thoughts, beliefs, and experiences that would have stopped you in the past and may still. This is not a process of applying labels of right and wrong ways to become enlightened. This is a process that is led by your I AM Self experienced through the filters of your personality. Gradually as the perceived world and the physical reality begin to line up, the views from your personality have less of a grip and you release your Self into the larger expression of your truth.

Your divine knowing is always at the helm, and your personality, through the filters of living in a physical realm, with history, memory, beliefs, fears, and worries, will step in front of the path set by your higher knowing. It is in moments where you think you have taken a step backward or face your own limitations that we encourage you to just stop. Breathe. Your truth already lies within your natural divine essence. From that perspective there is no wrong. Grant yourself some space to reorient to your knowing. Gather the clarity needed for your next steps. This may take moments or days. Be patient with yourself.

What is valuable here is the questioning and ultimate realization that patterns born of your personality are not your essential

Self. The experience may seem overwhelming, but the value of the questioning cannot be overstated. These are potent moments where you are recalibrating to your larger knowing. When you find situations, thoughts, and experiences you have drawn to yourself that no longer fit, the opportunity exists to re-choose consciously. In choosing, you take the potent stance of declaration available in the Now moment. Rather than following along in your life unconsciously, you have moved to a higher frequency where a broader perspective may be seen. You are increasing your perspective and frequency and elevating in vertical consciousness. You are living the edge of your known world and unknown realms. It is in this space that you hold the door open to what else is possible.

When you experience yourself in an emotional whirlwind, know that it is part of your plan to move from a state of unconsciousness to consciousness. It is your personality that frames events through the lens of right-wrong, good-bad, and in so doing limits the potential of each extraordinary moment from being seen. Your whirlwind, your bad day, your so-called collapse into unconsciousness is grist for the mill of your transformation.

Employ discernment to the best of your ability, allowing a recalibration to your ever-expanding reality. Grace is always present, as is the warm embrace of Love's inclusion. Choose to elevate your perspective.

DAY 261: ALIGNING VERSUS CONFORMING

Consider your soul's voice as the guiding beacon directing the events of your life. Your ability to hear the fine voice of your essential Self is the key, allowing high frequency realms of light and possibility to move with ease in your life. This is the dynamic of inner referencing. Living from the perspective of external referencing or conforming to external cues is part of the framework of collective consciousness. The unconscious experience of ease comes from fitting in, and a sense of familiarity that comes from past experience. The ongoing choice to move toward the unknown is a process that takes effort. On one hand there is the inner pull toward alignment with your divine nature, and on the other hand is experience in the material world that pushes you toward the collective. Today we assure you the effort is well placed to move toward your soul's voice.

There is a myriad of demands on your attention. When you live unconsciously it is easiest to fall into the default position of conforming to the framework of external referencing that supplies beliefs and values, without you thinking too much about it. As your conscious awareness expands, you choose consciously, determined by inner resonance. As you ask, "Is this a fit for me or is it not?" you create your life from a position of potency. Reassessing beliefs previously not questioned brings clarity to the process of inner referencing. As you choose to live in alignment with your divine essence, inner referencing is the only way.

Hallmarks of Internal Reference (Aligning Internally)

As you spend more moments in alignment with your essential Self, your frequency is naturally elevated. When you choose to live from the inside out, meaning you look inward for guidance, you are sourced by the light of your divine nature and you experience more:

Resonance
Vitality
Appreciation, Peace, Freedom, Clarity
Movement
Inspiration moving you to action
Discovery of your unique voice
Honoring of your essential Self
Wealth in all areas
Love

Hallmarks of External Reference (Conforming Externally)

Living a life of unconsciousness does not require you to be present. Living from the perspective of external referencing requires a denial of inner guidance and conformation to an external dynamic. The lure is an illusion of ease, because you are not taking responsibility for your life. Life experience in general is:

Ease of habit that doesn't require your presence
Lower frequency and vitality
Experience of and maintaining of status quo
Being "right" brings a sense of approval while furthering and affirming collective thought
Low inspiration (not challenged)
Depression, lack of involvement in life
Your soul's voice is not heard as you are sourced externally
Feeling something is missing: "There has to be more."

The feeling at the onset of the voyage of expanding awareness is one that requires more energy than perhaps you had been accustomed to expending. The reward, however, is Love itself. As you stay the course and resist conforming to the old patterns, you create a life of wholeness where your human nature is informed by your divine nature.

DAY 262: LOVE IS THE COMMON DENOMINATOR

Love is the impetus for All. The search for Love is the equalizing factor. It is the perception of Love that is unique, interpreted through the lens of each perspective. As an artist expresses their vision upon the canvas, each person expresses Love distinctly upon the canvas of their own life. Love is expressed through the frequency within which it is viewed.

A myopic perspective of Love is viewed externally, as in searching beyond Self for a person who, when found, completes them. This perspective implies an experience of Self as incomplete. The emphasis is upon Love as a physical and emotional external expression or need.

When viewed from a distant stance you begin to see that Love is the deep, abiding, eternal force that beckons you to look beyond the external expression to embrace your internal knowing. The view shifts from external to internal as you identify illusion and that which is not-Love. As not-Love is picked up, examined and placed back down, the definition of Love remains open, allowing space for Love to be discovered. As you distance yourself from the commonly held beliefs of Love, you employ an internal process of examining. The experience of resonance informs you beyond the external cues. It is then that the connection with your soul's wisdom may be activated.

Love, as the divine expression that encompasses All, that IS ALL, allows the highest expression of you to flourish. When you bring to bear *being* Love in your day's moments, the doors open to the universe's riches. Love's highest expression awaits.

DAY 263: EACH MOMENT

When you reside in the immaculate Now moment, you are ensconced within the space of Love, with the rich, high frequency experience of stillness, calm, and guidance of the highest order. We cannot emphasize enough the shift in your reality that is available within the immaculate moment of Now.

When you stand back, to gain a larger perspective, from the center of the Now moment, you recognize qualities sourced by your personality are not available. Your identity and personality are informed by experience in the material world and are not who you are as your essential Self. Have you noticed, for example, when you begin to meditate and quiet your mind, that your access to anger, or justification, is not present? The experience is one of a blank canvas, a place of being and openness in the moment. The myopic viewpoint of your personality becomes moot as you step back in perspective and begin to see from your expanded awareness. The larger your perspective, the more of your divine nature is allowed space, and the less your personality traits shroud your essence.

Qualities of your essential Self move to the forefront of your awareness as you BE present.

When you become an argument for your beliefs, you are unable to access possibility
beyond what you hold true.

Beliefs are formed from the past and close the door to potential held only in the Now moment. It is only as you are willing to look beyond the walls of your belief systems and the limited perceptions of your personality that you may find the treasure trove of possibility that is already you. Your process of enlightenment is about claiming your divine nature. When you cling to your limitations, only accessed through belief residing in the past or future, your highest expression is not available.

Your process of consciously expanding your awareness requires you to become proficient at shifting your perspective. The underlying implication is that you already hold a variety of perspectives and may consciously choose from the broad range of your ability. The blinders of unconsciousness are held in place with justification of one perspective and viewpoint over another. Blinders of unconsciousness hold in place the pain of separation, with each side debating the validity of their viewpoint. There is no meeting point available in debate. As you learn to step back and shift your perspective, you release the reins of a myopic viewpoint to engage the high frequency position of expanded awareness available only in the moment. Rather than meeting the limitations of a limited perspective with more of the same, you notice the perspective that is held. Rather than being an argument to be right, you see belief systems are held like security blankets enforcing a way of being and an absence of Self. This is the illusion.

The whole interplay of beliefs and personality viewed from the space of Now brings clarity that frees you from the fray of argument. The broad perspective available from your divine nature allows energy to be spent in expressing authentically rather than enforcing the bonds of unconsciousness.

The experience of the Now moment in and of itself is extraordinary. Your presence in the Now moment is the golden key for conscious access to your divine knowing. The Now moment is where you may access your divine knowing unhindered by the limitations of personality.

An empowered perspective is always available within the Now moment. Access the Now moment not through your doing but through your being. As Source in form, how vast is your awareness? Step back in perspective, release the bonds of beliefs from your personality. Embrace the light of your essence and step over the threshold of the Now moment to see newly.

DAY 264: RAISE YOUR FREQUENCY TO ACCESS YOUR DIVINE NATURE

The calm assurance and guidance of your highest knowing is always available. You make choices every moment about which level of awareness you occupy. The process of enlightenment allows those choices to be made consciously. As you practice the skills of shifting the density of your frequency, you take ownership of the vast expression that is authentically you. Available through your choice, you may move beyond the illusion of perceived limitations to access the unlimited potential that is yours.

With practice, raising your frequency is as easy as changing channels on your television. No longer feeling trapped or restricted with limited viewpoints, you may learn to dance the ladder of frequency with ease, purpose, and grace. As you access the higher frequencies that are authentically yours, you access new levels of awareness from higher-frequency perspectives. Instead of feeling overwhelmed or stopped by experience in the material world, you may choose a new perspective by accessing the higher frequency space of your divine nature. You hold the full spectrum of light from physical density to pure divine light, all is yours to access as you choose. As you begin to make new choices consciously, you open pathways to clarity and more ease, and open higher frequency access.

Our conversations support and catalyze awareness beyond the illusion of physical life, activating your divine nature. Considering the possibility of more is the key to seeking access.

Raise Your Frequency

- *Sit down and get comfortable. Hold your intention to access the fine frequency of your divine nature. Notice how you feel. If you have a current issue or problem you would like a new perspective on, hold that in your thoughts, or as a written note in your pocket. Realize that the resolution to any issue is not contained within the frequency of the problem. You must look to a higher frequency for perspective and solution. Innovation and original thought are available at high frequency states.*
- *Take 3 deep breaths. Call all parts of you to the present: "I bring all parts of me present here and Now. I bring all parts of me present here and Now. I bring all parts of me present here and Now." You may ask your Council of Light to be present as well to support your experience.*
- *Intend to shift your perspective by raising your frequency.*
- *Feel a spacious cylinder of white light that surrounds you vertically, extending high above you. The frequency you currently occupy at the bottom of the cylinder represents the density of your human expression.*
- *Viewed as layers, you see increasingly fine layers of frequency above you. Intend to float up into the finer layers of your light expression. As you rise up within the expansive cylinder of light, feel yourself releasing the density of layers below you. You must release something in order to rise to the next higher level. You do not need to identify what you are leaving behind, just intend to hold the highest level of your divine light presence. You may visualize taking things out of a suitcase or rising in a hot air balloon and releasing ballast as you rise higher (my personal favorite).*
- *Feel your movement upward within the cylinder of light that is all you. As you rise, feel the density remaining below you. You begin to feel lighter. Your frequency is rising.*
- *Whether you rise a little or a lot, notice your new perspective. Stay for a moment and recalibrate to the new frequency. Breathe. Notice how natural and unencumbered the finer frequency feels. Notice a new perspective that is available.*

- *If you would like to look at the issue you brought with you, remove the note from your pocket and now, from a clean slate, observe what arises in your awareness. As you feel comfortable, you may expand your time in this elevated awareness. Feel the natural and expansive space you are within. Initially you may feel a little light-headed, so allow time to calibrate, and when you are ready, choose to return to a frequency that feels comfortable and stabilized for what you need to do in your day. Be responsible with your choices; for example, you wouldn't choose to access an elevated frequency while your physical presence is needed to drive.*

- *When you are ready, take another deep breath and return to a frequency that is comfortable. Notice what you notice. You understand now how you may choose your way of being. You may choose your perspective. You know where to go to BE the fine frequency of your essential Self.*

The more you practice the art of divine access, the better you become and the easier you transition from one frequency to another by choice. Your ability to stay within a high frequency will depend upon your ability to sustain an unencumbered, broad perspective without reaching for the past or what you think you know. You will find how reflexive low frequency presence really is.

If you are a musician or an artist, or hold any other type of passionate creative expression, realize you are already accessing the timeless, high frequency space of inspiration. All this is to claim the experience and perspective of your expansive divine nature, which is already who you are. When you integrate your divine nature with your human experience you claim your wholeness.

This you do naturally already. Our conversations support unconscious knowing moved to the light of your awareness.

DAY 265: ANOTHER LOOK

Today, we revisit a model of consciousness introduced in *In Service to Love Book 1: Love Remembered*. The purpose is to bring a dynamic into view that allows you, from where you sit now, to continue moving beyond limitation. The ability to traverse varying levels of awareness with no loss of potency allows for a greater bandwidth of expression.

If you can hold a broad view of this consciousness dynamic, you will notice that the emotional weight of whatever life situation lies before you is taken off the table, and empowering choice is returned. The concept today is clarity regarding horizontal consciousness and vertical consciousness.

Horizontal Consciousness

Imagine living on a lower-floor apartment and your life only consists of what is around you. You develop a myopic viewpoint informed only by what you see. Mastery of this level of consciousness is dependent upon getting more familiar with your external environment.

Consider that horizontal consciousness maintains a status quo, valuing only the priorities of the collective consciousness. The collective is a template for separation consciousness, which values external expertise over inner knowing. In the priorities of collective consciousness, the individual is not valued above the collective's mandate. Change is slow, because high frequency innovation, beyond the lower frequency expression of the collective, is not supported. The experience for most is one of fitting in. The brass ring is displayed outwardly in material gain. Mastery in this level of consciousness is how well you play the game. As external cues take the reins the skills for inner referencing are not valued or acknowledged. Self-awareness is not identified as supportive of attaining mastery. This level of consciousness demonstrates separation, setting the stage for opposition, power, and control. The frequency range that contains horizontal consciousness is limited to lower levels because there is no value given to inner awareness or access to high frequency states of being. Lifetimes may be spent in this cycle of consciousness.

There is value in experiencing the contrast of life. Separation consciousness and horizontal consciousness are valuable in the soul journey.

Understand that horizontal consciousness may also be expressed at higher frequencies as the position at the edge of known and unknown realms is relinquished. For many, their rise of frequency above the collective will bring a respite from the density of human nature but also not advance ultimate awareness. In other words, horizontal consciousness may also represent a stagnation of sorts that resides at higher frequency levels above the level of collective consciousness.

Vertical Consciousness

Imagine living at the top of a tall skyscraper. Your vantage point allows greater perspective on your life. You see the power of perspective and take responsibility for your greatest authentic expression. Issues prevalent in horizontal consciousness are surmountable, and myopic limitations are moot. Mastery from this perspective is unlimited as you access your nonlinear essence and are informed by your unlimited Self as you continue to lean into the realms of the unknown.

From a vertical consciousness standpoint, you not only access information available from your human nature but hold a broader perspective that allows you to see the limitations inherent in your humanity. From your vast perspective in the Now moment you see the broad range of your innate ability as you turn your attention toward your nonlinear or divine nature. Your human nature once viewed as your totality is now only seen as a small part of who you ARE. As Source in form, you take ownership of and responsibility for your wholeness.

Vertical consciousness is equally available and not as easily seen. The journey of vertical consciousness is a description of the path less taken. In the paradigm of vertical consciousness, the expression is upward, seeking inner wisdom and at the same time releasing the density of restriction. The search is for the more that exists beyond the limitations of the physical.

You are within a vertical consciousness paradigm. The values of vertical consciousness are reflected through exploration of inner realms and inspiration. The process of vertical awareness is initiated through inner promptings, not external values. It is in times such as the transition from separation consciousness to unity consciousness that the movement on the vertical scale of consciousness is highly supported as the weight or density of physical experience is lifted. Still, the treasure available through vertical consciousness is open to all who seek. Within this paradigm, limitations of physical experience are seen allowing empowered choice. The door opens to choose yet again between separation consciousness and unity consciousness. The process of movement on the vertical consciousness axis is through empowered choice in every moment. Vertical consciousness seeks beyond the limitations of physical reality into the inspiration, wisdom, and clarity available through divine nature. Integration of human nature and divine nature is a natural evolutionary step. Only when ready, as internally directed, will someone seek vertical consciousness. The frequency range of this state of consciousness is high, as you are sourced internally by the potency of Love.

You see the movement of the collective consciousness around you every day. You see those who have chosen mastery of the physical realm. As though your expanded reality doesn't exist, they do not hold the ability to see beyond their choice for physical mastery. You, as an explorer into the realms of light, may not be seen, but then again, you are internally directed, no longer needing the affirmation of others.

We bring up this topic at this time to create a new level of clarity. As you move on the gradient scale of expression your relationship to all things physical shifts. Ways of connecting with those who have chosen different paths are shifting—not that one path is better than another. The ability for others to see all of you is limited by their own choice for consciousness, either vertical or horizontal. This perspective opens a new space for being as your process of expansion continues.

As ever, we are,
In Service to Love

DAY 266: BEYOND

The awareness that becomes possible as you move along the path of enlightenment is a heightened experience. You begin to see beyond the limitations and edges of the physical world, and a broader reality comes into focus. The experiences you had once felt as hard and fast, as beyond argument in their reality, become more diffuse with realms of contributing factors. The reality once seen as indisputable is far larger and more mysterious when experienced from the perspective of your divine, multidimensional capacity.

The new expanded awareness is not only one that searches beyond what is visible but then deeply appreciates, within the Now moment, the magnificence, beauty, and intricacy of the physical experience. As your awareness expands you create from a larger expression of your being than was available before. You not only see the divine expressions around you, but you BE the highest expression available as an outcome of your wholeness. Your contribution in light is greater than what is seen. The emanations of your divine expression ripple throughout your life, contribute to those you encounter, and to the well-being of All. As the vitality of one tree contributes to the vitality of the whole forest and exponentially expands the collective expression, so do you.

We invite you to bask in the beauty that surrounds your day and the Love of those around you. Consider that with each magnificent moment of appreciation you contribute to the expression of Love available for All. Your footsteps on the path of what is beyond the physical brings divine potential realized into the physical realms. And beyond.

DAY 267: COURAGE TO BE SEEN

Good afternoon, dearest Beloveds, it is I, Thoth, stepping to the forefront of this divine conversation today within this Now immaculate moment. As you expand your awareness and access the bandwidth sourced by your light, you grow in expression. As a tree starts as a seedling and expands to fulfill the divine design that is ever present, the tree becomes more beautiful. Unable to hide under the canopy of the forest, the maturing tree reaches great heights, revealing the magnificence of the divine design actualized. And so it is with you.

Those present in light today support your expanding expression of Love as it emanates your exquisite I AM. Stepping to the forefront of today's conversation are Jeshua, Archangel Michael, Archangel Gabriel, Isis, Mary Magdalene, Infinite Oneness, Melchizadek, Metatron, and St. Germain.

We bring this to your attention today to affirm the actualization of your true nature. You are exquisite. As you continue to take on the light that is your essential Self, your brilliance may not be hidden. Distinct from others who are burdened beneath the coverings of the limitations of physical experience, you start to stand out. The anonymity that comes with flying below the radar is in direct opposition to your true nature. Your presence is no longer neutral. Your presence is declarative.

This brings up reactions at times from others who, not familiar with their own authentic nature, have no basis for understanding yours. Remember, this is a voyage of inner direction. As you leave the need for external affirmation in the rearview mirror, understand that, equal to your expansion, your inner direction reigns.

Today we support your ongoing process of expansion and fulfillment of the magnificence of your divine design with an infusion of light, if you so choose. We amplify the strength of your light expression, stabilizing your stance. We will work with you, clearly supporting the integration process of the light you possess.

With ease and grace for all your systems, your stance within the newly reached light expression paves the way for what is to come; the manifestation of your essential nature, revealed one step at a time.

In Love, with Love, from Love,
The Council of Light

Day 268: Elevate Awareness to Movement as a New Normal

You are the conductor of the masterpiece that is your life. Each note, each choice, represents an inner-directed action. As you elevate the awareness that you hold, a new expression becomes available beyond a previous baseline way of being. Your access to the new bandwidth of frequencies requires your ongoing presence.

This is not an automatic type of shift. Adjusting to living with a broader awareness requires consciousness to access it. Remember, you are no longer living on autopilot within a normal and expected way of being. Rather than having only moments of expanded awareness that reside beyond your normal range of living, consciously shift your awareness to encompass the expanded and higher frequency range you know you possess. As your consciousness is raised, you naturally receive more information. Rather than relying on your past version of normal as the way to navigate your day, elevate your frequency yet again to access the part of your knowing that accesses even greater bandwidths of light.

You will find that there is a mismatch, a disconnect, or a lack of resonance that will occur as you expect your past way of being to work for you now as you hold a broader range of awareness. The fact is, your awareness has outgrown your previous perspective. So, too, does your way of being require a new set point or baseline. The higher set point is achieved through the intention to create a new set point as a way of being. The higher frequency set point accesses your expanded awareness. The set point does not automatically change. It is birthed from a complex set of unconscious decisions and now requires movement from unconscious to conscious awareness. Have you found a sense of malaise or lower energy of late? This is due to a misaligning of a default way of being during your day. The default is the way you are being when you aren't thinking about it. As you continue to expand, as you are never still, your presence is required to a greater extent in your life, because you are now living consciously, not absently.

There is a natural reflex to retreat a bit, especially after a significant amount of expansion. That is natural. Consider that your previous default way of being no longer is expansive enough to access the fuel you need for your day. You are now sourced by your divine essence. So, as you get ready in the morning, intend to increase your frequency and run at a new, higher frequency during your day. You will sense the weight of the past, the weight of worry, the weight of exhaustion, lift and give you room to move with ease during your day with greater presence.

It is in Love that we meet you.

Day 269: Holding Your Center

Good evening, dearest Beloveds, it is I, Thoth, moving into the forefront of this divine conversation, within this Now immaculate moment. As you move into the expanded state of awareness, the details that used to move past you are caught in your attention. It is easy to move to the space of reacting to the seeming increase in the flow of information. Rather, what is called for within the paradigm of unity consciousness is the skill of holding your center. Those present this evening in light include many more than are named. Moving to the forefront of this conversation is Jeshua, Melchizadek, Infinite Oneness, Legions of Light, Mary Magdalene, Archangel Gabriel, and Archangel Michael.

The increase in your sensitivity calls for adaptation to the new experience of what-is-so. This is distinct from our conversation last night about recalibrating a new set point as your dominant frequency. This is distinct in that, regardless of your frequency choice, the skill of returning to your center becomes more relevant as a selfcare strategy and as a way to continue expanding your awareness. The ability to move to your center is a way you respond to your environment in the moment. It is through reaction that you unconsciously jump to a patterned way of being. Patterned ways of being are unconscious for the most part. Our work together, our divine collaboration, is all about bringing what is unconscious to a level of consciousness. As you do, you have the opportunity to bring the knowing you hold at your highest expression into any situation in your life.

In a world that is changing quickly, your ability to hold a place of centered awareness becomes key. This evening we offer a strategy to re-center. First of all, when you find yourself in a place of unconscious being or in a state of reaction, these are red flags that signal you have moved off your center point. As you hold an intention to stay centered, you will notice your reactions will gradually deintensify with practice. You will begin to notice a reactionary situation before you are in the middle of it and then center yourself rather than react. It is from a centered space that you have the opportunity to respond, rather than react in reflex.

Holding Your Center: A Practice

As you expand your conscious awareness, hold the intention to receive and <u>allow</u> the high frequency information that is now within reach. The choice for full consciousness is a choice for wholeness. When you employ unity consciousness, you give up the divisiveness of separation consciousness. You choose wholeness. When you choose to align with your highest knowing, your knowing is reached through the centered experience of the Now moment. Reaction is a function of past or future. Within reaction, responding is not available. Responding requires a position within the Now.

The fastest way to the Now and then also to your center is through your breath. Take three deep breaths. Declare internally or externally, if possible, "I bring all parts of my being present here and Now!" Note: This is a declaration. It is said with meaning and a sense of commandment. You are a master creator. The information and wisdom that resides within your highest expression is not reached by being wishy-washy. Create clarity by being clear! Connecting with nature is a way to move yourself to the Now moment. Look at the colors of the sky, the clouds, the leaves, the birds, the butterfly beside you. Visualize yourself as fully connected to All.

Visualize your space of centeredness. It is a space of extraordinary comfort, beauty, and connection to your essential Self. The space of center evokes your most empowered, connected way of being. In the past, it was these profound moments that were noticed because they were different from your habitual way of being. We suggest that the space of profound connection is a platform for access to your divine expression, manifested. Visualize your space of centeredness; feel it throughout your body. Once you feel yourself within your space of centeredness, take a deep breath and exhale. As you exhale, imagine you are expanding the bubble of centeredness around you. You hold space within your center. The breathing into your center to expand it is a way of amplifying your experience. So rather than feeling "thin" or "light" within the space of center, you feel solid and robust. Again, there is a sense of commanding here.

Hold your space of centeredness as long as you can. If you fall off or out of center, let it be. This is not another reason to be hard on yourself. It is a bit like learning to ride a bike. Once you get the sense of balance within this space, you will be able to re-create it whenever you choose. That is the point of this exercise. You may choose the space of your center at any time.

It is in the space of center that you may begin to consciously access the beauty that is yours. Beyond the expressions that have been available so far. What if you could live your life from moments of profound connection? What could become possible?

In Love, with Love, from Love,
The Council of Light

DAY 270: TO TOUCH THE SACRED

Good evening, dearest Beloveds. It is I, Thoth, moving to the forefront of this divine conversation within this Now immaculate moment. As you expand your awareness into the light expression of your true nature, you behold the sacred. This evening we set the space for sacred connection with your divine knowing. We set the space for what is to come, if you so choose. As your awareness expands and you move that which had been subconscious to conscious awareness, you experience your own sacred being. Those in light standing by your side support your expansion of awareness so you may see, perhaps for the first time, the truth of your divine expression. You are accompanied this evening by Jeshua, Melchizadek, Mary Magdalene, Isis, Legions of Light, Sanat Kumara, the Council of the Golden Heart, Archangel Michael, Archangel Gabriel, the Grandmothers, the Grandfathers, Gaia.

The elevated moments of experience are not planned, not prepared for; they happen in the Now moment. The rarefied air of the ecstatic moment bathes you in the Love and light of your authentic nature. Not something outside you, these moments of touching the sacred greet you eye to eye and heart to heart. You are embraced as the Beloved. As you touch the sacred you may give way to the gentle caress of Love's intoxication.

When you find yourself in these moments of ecstatic bliss and beauty, realize that you are beholding You. You behold Love's expression, imbued with the perfection only you may bring. We remind you of the perfection of you, elevating your experience to open the door, to cross the threshold, into the next space of your awareness. Always a choice, the experience is more Love, more beauty, more of You. You, as your most potent expression, are realized and actualized. As you view the most breathtaking moments, you inhale the divine. The light of the clouds across the sky this evening is impeccable. The beauty is unspeakable. This is the reflection of You.

We hold you in the intoxicatingly beautiful truth of you. When you touch the space of the sacred, breathe in the exquisite beauty that is you. I AM that I AM.

Beautiful. In Love, with Love, from Love,
The Council of Light

DAY 271: RISING INTO YOUR HIGHEST EXPRESSION

Good evening, dearest Beloveds. It is I, Thoth, stepping to the forefront of this divine conversation within this Now immaculate moment. As you elevate your way of being, you move toward alignment with your Christed-Self. The ascension process describes your soulful journey to wholeness. As you take on more of the divine light that is your true nature, you BE-come. You become more informed by your divine nature and less by your human nature. You hold the light and fine frequency deeply connected to your most sacred expression. You, as Love, become more of who you are and less of who you are not. When you align with your divine essence as a fundamental way of being you bring the grace, Love, compassion, and wisdom assigned to the Master who walked in form 2,000 years ago. You bring that and more through your own unique expression available on the earth star Now.

Moving to the forefront of this conversation this evening are those who support you in your Christed presence available Now, including Jeshua, Mary Magdalene, Archangel Gabriel, Archangel Michael, Melchizadek, Infinite Oneness, Legions of Light, and St. Germain. The Christed expression is available to all who seek. This refers to the mastery that is attainable while in form. Only attainable through the alignment with your divine essence. When one aligns with the potent divine essence that is beyond all limitations, you experience the ecstatic essence of Love and are informed by the most-high expression of your being. The manifestation is one that occurs within the Now immaculate moment at the point of creation: pure potential made manifest. We speak of this today to remind you of the potential that lies within you and that is available as you choose. Through the stories of the Holy Bible and other teachings, the works of Jesus were held as miraculous. We say to you, "You are where miraculous resides."

At this point of *In Service to Love* we begin to set the stage for a new way of being that is less hindered by the limitations of form and more authentic to you than any other way of being. Able to live within the state of physical form and yet beyond it, you exercise your multidimensional capacity with ease and grace. Your divine expression of Love that is uniquely yours becomes manifest. With the high frequency that it holds, your aligned presence transforms. Your presence is alchemical.

As you choose, we light the path illuminating the next step that lies before you. At each moment we follow your choice and honor you in this process as the divine Master you are. What is it to live from, "I AM that I AM"?

Within the state of "I AM" resides the profound.

In Love, with Love, from Love,
The Council of Light

DAY 272: MOVING FORWARD

Good evening, dearest Beloveds. It is I, Thoth, moving to the forefront of this divine conversation within this Now immaculate moment. In the process of expanding awareness, as you choose moving forward into the experience of more of you, you experience an ever-broadening perspective. As you feel the movement forward, you shed the skin of the old way of being in favor of what is to come. This is a day of acknowledging how far you have moved and looking at what is now available. Present in light today are Jeshua, Mary Magdalene, Infinite Oneness, St. Germain, White Brotherhood, Legions of Light, Elohim, Archangel Gabriel, and Archangel Michael.

Today we make the distinction between two perspectives to engage transformation. Consider that there is a middle ground where you intend transformation yet are not acting upon it. By gaining clarity about your own process you may bring patience, ease, and compassion to your Self.

1. *Your perspective is directed by the <u>thought</u> of being exposed to new information, yet there is no appreciable difference in the way that life is lived from the Now moment. Life's choices idle in what has been.*

2. *Your perspective is one of <u>engaging</u> the transformation. Life's experiences shift and move in accordance with the new perspectives that are utilized as a lens through which to view the world and your view of yourself. Life choices engage what is possible in the Now moment.*

Both choices are perfect. The point of this conversation is to become aware of how you unconsciously think about change. It is easy to talk about, but the *reality* of movement is challenging for your human nature. It is supportive to notice where you are. If you are choosing to engage transformation, you find that your life is changing, and you are experiencing expansion of your expression in light, which brings to the surface an awareness of limitations that were previously unconscious. It takes focus, intention, and courage to choose movement forward as your awareness actually shifts. The choice for expanding consciousness is not passive.

We bring these up today to distinguish which space you are in at this point and to identify areas where there is resistance. The feeling of resistance may be an opportunity to look for limitations that are present, or default ways of being that have not yet surfaced consciously.

This is not a process that you "grind" through. This is a new way of being that utilizes your joy as fuel and your curiosity as a blank canvas for inspiration. In any case, however you feel about the experience of change, we ask you to contemplate how you BE in change. As you move to the finer frequencies of your light expression, your resistance, the resistance you have always had to change, will be challenged. Be with the clarity you receive and allow a new way of being to surface in your awareness. As you move on the gradient scale of light expression, the ways of being hold more ease, beauty, joy, acknowledgment, compassion, and connection.

The snake sheds the outer skin as it no longer fits the expansion that is available. You too are shedding the skin of the limitations of the past to allow space for the experience of your divine design.

In Love, with Love, from Love,
The Council of Light

Day 273: Translating Light into Conscious Awareness

Good evening, dearest Beloveds. It is I, Thoth, moving to the forefront of this divine conversation within this Now immaculate moment. As you move on the gradient scale of light expression you begin to gather more information, perceived through light. You have always been receiving through light. It is truly your nature. Walking the path of enlightenment brings conscious awareness to the process, enabling a clear and aligned communication informed by your I AM presence. As your conscious reach moves into the higher realms of light, you become aware of more detail in your day, as you perceive beyond the five known senses. It seems, now, that you absorb information through all parts of your being. The information you receive may be discerned with a higher level of detail, beyond an influx of feeling and sensing.

You are learning a new language of light. The awareness available in light is potent and holds greater depth and expanse, because resistance, or static, has been released. As you sift and sort through your beliefs, habits, and patterns, you clear the pathway to receiving more from your essential Self. There is less distortion experienced as the information you receive in light is freed of the fundamental limitations of human experience. In essence, as you loosen yourself from the bonds of the collective consciousness of separation, you may hear more freely the truth of your own divine voice.

As you develop a curiosity around what may be contained within your own soul's communication, and that of your Council of Light, you may further fine-tune your awareness. Imagine a ball of yarn of many colors. At first glance, there is no rhyme or reason. With further observation you find there is perfection in the order of color, sequence, and frequency. The information is also perceived through sensing beyond the ability to think. Beyond thinking, an osmosis occurs, a permeating of the light information into your being. Are you more responsive lately to thought? Sound? Color? Physical sensation? Knowing? Visual cues in nature? Look beyond your ability to think. Become curious about how you process information beyond your ability to think it.

You have been experiencing this process in an accelerated format through *In Service to Love* and our divine collaboration. As you sit with the intention of clarity and the question of how you naturally work with light information, allow the answer to rise within you. It will be a gentle awareness brought in by the tide of your being.

We celebrate your expanding awareness and the clarity now possible in light. As you seek counsel with your own divine essence, all heaven sings.

Day 274: Honoring Your Great Journey

Good evening, dearest Beloveds. It is I, Thoth, stepping to the forefront of this divine conversation within this Now immaculate moment. The turbulent energies that are present on the planet Earth right now represent the turning of the tide of conscious awareness. Those at the leading edge of transformation herald a new way of being for All. You, as leaders in the evolution of Love, usher in the reality of a new paradigm. We step back today to present the vast perspective that we see. As beings of light in light, our mission is to support yours. As Emissaries of Love, you carry the message of Love's freedom within the radiance you emit.

The presence in light this evening is vast beyond counting. Those who step forward to lend their name to the process of *In Service to Love* represent thousands of beings in light, also holding the torch for Love's light to spread to the far reaches of creation. Present at the forefront of this gathering today are Jeshua, Melchizadek, Metatron, Mary Magdalene, Isis, White Brotherhood, Council of the Golden Heart, Council of Nine, Sanat Kumara, Council of Thirteen, Archangel Michael, Archangel Gabriel, the Hathors, and Legions of Light.

The message today comes from all reaches of the multiverse. As you embrace the brilliance of your own light, you emit your divine emanation of Love. The force for Love that you are transforms beyond your capabilities of understanding. Love's pure essence is potent, as the limitations found in the experience of physical form are released. You move far beyond the distractions of your daily life to pursue what is sourced from your I AM Self. You are inspired through your soul's divine mission of Love. Your mission is uniquely expressed as the details of your life unfold. The stage you stand upon is vast. As you have the courage to look at your own limitations, rather than being bogged down by the experience you continue to move forward, gathering the courage to be who you have always been. You are also fueled by the hope, the intention, the possibility that others may see the brilliance of their own divine expression, so they too may fulfill the highest intention of their sacred essence.

We gather today to extend our expression of Love to you in acknowledgment of your undertaking to stand in the brilliance of Love's pure light. We witness the alchemical qualities of your interactions, seemingly simple, but potent as transformative catalysts. As you hold the courage to approach Love through your experience in form, you come face-to-face with what is not-Love, yet hold the courage to champion a journey that exists beyond the sight of others.

We affirm your steps of Love and compassion. Each difficult day, each moment of your own transformative process, heals realms you don't see. This is not an easy path. As leaders, you confront in each step an argument for stagnation and default. Your actions in the name of Love birth the new earth into form. The new earth holds the highest frequencies now available through the evolutionary process into unity consciousness.

What seems like the argument for Love's grace at the forefront of collective consciousness heralds the great awakening of humanity. From our perspective, as Masters of Love in light, you are held on high, in reverence, and are buoyed by our Love.

We are an alliance of Love's freedom and sacred promise, in Service to Love.

DAY 275: WELCOME HOME

A Prayer of Abundance

I allow Love's abundance to reign over me.
Ever present to blessings, I stand in the light of Love
And say, "Yes!"
And so it is.

Dearest Beloveds, it is I, Thoth, stepping to the forefront of this divine conversation within this Now immaculate moment. As you move on the gradient scale of light, your environment shifts. Expressions that were not available in the presence of limitations now open as not only possible, but as manifestations of your authentic divine nature. As you move on the gradient scale of light there are new keys, new signposts, that are increasingly powerful.

Those present in light this afternoon sit with you as you integrate the eternal knowing of light into your conscious awareness and the physical experience. Moving to the forefront of today's conversation are your own Council of Light, Jeshua, Infinite Oneness, Mary Magdalene, Isis, Archangel Gabriel, Archangel Michael, the Elohim, and White Brotherhood.

Dearest Beloveds, as you increase capacity consciously to move in the finer light realms of your essential Self, your physical experience must shift to include the expanding awareness you hold in light. The markers or signposts of being in an expanded space of light now are different than your understanding at earlier stages. Imagine being on the edge of a pool and the experience there. Now imagine yourself within the pool. The experience in the water is different. Your environment is wet, you have new sensory experiences, your movement changes to accommodate the qualities of your surroundings. And so it is with your experience in an expanded spaciousness of light expression. Rather than comparing your experience in light to your known definitions of previous experience, notice the qualities of your light expression newly. Reach into resonance and your knowing in light for clarity.

You are uncovering your own divine nature that has always existed in light. Our conversation today opens an empowered perspective to occur that serves you greatly for your next steps forward. Do you see that? When you compare life events to your school experience in elementary school, it is not large enough to include your knowing that occurs in college. At the completion of your master's degree, you see the perfection of each stage and the contribution it brings. Being in the moment of your expanding awareness, beyond comparisons and definitions of past experience, allows your expansive nature freedom for expression.

Welcome

We have been asking you to center yourself by saying, "I bring all parts of me present here and now." We make a note here. You will be bringing all parts of you present. This includes parts that were separated through the trauma of life events. If you notice yourself experiencing unexpected fear, concern, and anxiety, consider that a part of you that has come forward may be a part that holds those expressions and was separated. So, when you say, "I bring all parts of me present here and now," make a special consideration for parts of you that separated out of pain. They have returned. Welcome them home. Welcome all parts of you into Love's embrace. You will notice the increased potency that comes from your own integration and experience of wholeness. Welcome all parts of you home to the safe haven of Love.

Present in Love, All heals.

In Love, with Love, from Love,
The Council of Light

DAY 276: RAISED ON HIGH

Good evening, dearest Beloveds. It is I, Thoth, standing before you as representative, delivering the voice of the beings of light in light in alliance with you in your endeavor to become the Love that is your true nature. The gatherings in light are increasingly vast. As we move deeper into the light that is available, you have risen to take your place at the table, participating not only as a student but as a member of the Council of Light. Up to this point within *In Service to Love*, we have presented ourselves by name, in part so that you begin to become aware of the shifting frequencies that are available in light. This has given you a method of measuring, identifying, or bookmarking specific frequencies within the messages delivered. At this point your reach into light is significant. Moving forward we shift to acknowledging the presence of the Council of Light in the expanding and shifting expression as a collective of Love whose voice is in unison. The messages will contain particular notes or frequencies that are catalysts for specific levels of awareness determined in the Now moment.

The reason for this shift in presentation is to acknowledge the action of today. You are "raised on high." You hold access to finer frequencies now. Your limitations and density have lifted and no longer represent a block for your expression. This is a new step in the moving forward of your intention to embody that which is your divine expression. Your intention, your actions, and the synchronistic activities of Gaia within the evolutionary portal that is now present all play a part in the actions of today.

The process of moving upon the gradient scale of light expression so far has been about the capabilities, choice, and action for the realities of transformation. Moving your reality from one of density to one of light is lifetimes in the making. Beyond the limitations of beliefs, you have chosen truth. Truth is seen as wholeness viewed from a vast perspective. Your willingness to see beyond the veil of collective illusion opens the door to Love's healing for All.

Your reach into the light expression of your divine truth is within your grasp. Unburdened by the weight of illusion, you may soar to the heights of your soul's vision. We support you in voicing the ecstatic song of Love only you may sing. You are now remembering the language in light that is your first language.

Today you are raised on high. A celebration. An acknowledgment. A declaration of Love's eternal embrace of you.

In Love, with Love, from Love,

The Council of Light

DAY 277: BEYOND TRAJECTORY

We have often referred to the trajectory of your ascension process. The concept of trajectory is an important one. It holds within it an implication of moving from one place to another. Trajectory evokes a picture of a line; with a beginning and a direction of movement. There is the insinuation as well that you are moving into a space of greater expression, and the movement is propelled beyond your action at some point, gaining a level of momentum and then velocity.

We are at a point in expansive awareness when the analogy of trajectory has shifted slightly. There is a point in your expanding awareness when the relationship to the linear life experience does not match up with the perspective, depth, texture, wisdom, history, and possibility you access in the space of light. In essence you now cannot un-remember your own capacity in light.

Consider the process, both arduous and joyous, up to the top of the mountain. Now what becomes available? The experience at the pinnacle is greater than pictures may ever relay. Encapsulated into the experience is every step it has taken to get there. And now you have arrived in a new, rarefied space. Recognize that you may not feel you have accomplished this task. The answer is yours. What we relay in today's message is the shift in reality that occurs while you are on the way. All of a sudden, you are there. "But I don't feel any different. How could that be?" Consider that the reality of light is one that operates beyond the capabilities of thinking. As you move on the gradient scale of light expression your light has been shining more brightly. You have crossed a myriad of thresholds that have only become available as you move beyond what has been, in search of the greatest expression of you and in answer to the calling of your deepest voice. Consider your ability in light as it is Now. You have arrived at a new pinnacle of awareness.

We move from the visualization of trajectory at this point to indicate a new way of being that is now available. Beyond the linear expression you have mastered within the physical experience, there is the sacred revelation of your divine design and what that means within your physical experience. No longer moving in a straight line toward something, you have moved more deeply into the experience of light. Rather than thinking of your process of expanding awareness as moving from one space to another, we ask you to now consider your journey as a process of revealing the truth of you.

The expansive truth of you is a hard concept to grasp. The experience of your truth is one that resides in light. You have moved far enough along the gradient scale of light expression now to access your multidimensional awareness. Is there anything for you to do? No, just BE. Make potent choices around your being. "Today, I choose to be clarity." "Today, I choose to be beauty." "Today I choose to be wisdom." You will notice your capacity to create from your expression of being has increased. Choose who you be and then be present in your day. Follow your joy and direction from inspiration. Learn to listen to your heart's melody.

This is a space where your thinking is not always helpful. As life knows how to live, trust your inner knowing; your innate expression is the divine light of Love. Love transforms. Love is a catalyst. Feel your expansive expression Now. Allow the brilliance of your innate being to bring you the awareness at the most perfect moment. This shift in awareness allows you to hold an even greater perspective.

DAY 278: YOUR HIGHEST EXPRESSION

Conscious awareness has been the intention of many seekers over the millennia. You, in past incarnations, have spent lifetimes yearning for the match, while you were in form, that would resonate with the deep, inner calling of your soul.

Consider that this time, this Now moment, is the greatest expression of any of your previous incarnations. Now you are beyond the reach of most to understand. Yet that is no longer your motivation. You have turned your ear inward to hear the beat of your heart and the whispers of your greatest knowing. Able to bridge the worlds of the physical, balanced with your knowing in light, you are developing your mastery of being.

The journey to this level of knowing is not reached by many. The level of knowing at this stage is referred to as realization. Realization moved into action is actualization, the manifestation of that which is informed by your I AM presence.

We, as beings of light in light, support you as your touchstones within the vast expanse of Love's expression. When you begin to feel your feet lift off the ground, know for sure that you are capable of mastering All of your being. Whether you're going to a baseball game or the grocery store, or meditating and experiencing the bliss of ecstatic connection, you are All of it. From one end of the spectrum to the other. One brilliant, glorious expression of Love.

You have found your way through the field of illusion to the doors of I AM. What could possibly happen Now?

Day 279: Stepping into the Light of Your Own Empowerment

Within every Now moment, you have an opportunity to think, Be, and choose newly. As you are occupying more time within the space of high frequency awareness, you continue to make choices beyond the density of separation consciousness into the brilliance of your divine expression. Today we speak of what becomes available as you reach your own empowerment and gather the potency within your wholeness. What does empowerment look like from the perspective of enlightenment?

You have stepped over the threshold of limitation into the treasure trove of greater wisdom, Love, grace, peace, joy, abundance, compassion, and more. This movement in light calls for a reorientation to empowerment. What do you consider powerful? Whom do you consider powerful? Today, your Scribe noticed our presence as powerful, almost forceful, in strength and potency. We would say we are demonstrating clarity of intention. We ask you to consider your *being* in relation to what you deem powerful. Your empowered presence is a reflection of your integrated human nature and divine nature.

Our movement in light with Darlene in preparation for today's writing was experienced as powerful, swift, with clear direction, intention, and declaration. A demonstration of empowerment that is a match for divine expression. It is this level of clarity in declaration that we ask you to consider. First of all, what in your life do you declare? What is important to you? Realize your potency not only in creating but from the point of choice that first directs the creation. Where is there a level of default, or a demonstration of neutrality that is only so because you have not chosen? The choices you make when you occupy the level of light that is now available to you consciously are potent. Each choice in alignment with your true nature supports more being that is in alignment with your true nature. This is a potent way of being. We bring an example from your Scribe today. She noticed low level fears or concerns arise. She wrestled with them over a few hours, until she realized that was not in alignment with her true nature. She then declared that she stood in the space of her highest expression. From this space, nothing has control over her.

When fears are present, their presence indicates that power has been given to them. Realign with your divine nature and all else in your creation assumes a new perspective. The more time you spend in the light of your truth, the more you begin to realign into your authentic expression of empowerment. You see more clearly the moments where you have assigned something or someone dominion over you.

When you feel yourself in a space that is not honoring or empowering, take a deep breath and take two steps "up" or "to the side" to align with your true nature. As if you were stepping out of the shadows, into the brilliance of your truth, step into the light of your potency.

Your empowerment is not a space of acquiring power. As you remove limitations that are not your truth, you move beyond the old perceptions of power to begin to see your Self newly. Informed by your I AM, your potency is a natural way of being that is clear, direct, unlimited, and unwavering in Love.

And so it is.

DAY 280: MOTIVATED BY LOVE

*There is no space for your fear to stand when you are aligned with
the light of your divine being.*

As you integrate more of your knowing and wisdom that is held
in light, it is appropriate to sift and sort through ways of being
that show up during your day and look at them anew, through the
lens of Love.

When you began the process of expanding consciousness, you
started to integrate new thoughts and concepts into your awareness. As with a diamond, when you shift to a new facet a new reflection is seen. As you have gently turned the facets of your being,
more information has been added to your awareness that in turn
asks for choice in each moment. You begin to move what was
unconscious into your conscious territory. With promptings from
your deepest being, rather than holding a limited focus you have
opened to the vast possibility and potential that is your authentic
nature.

As you have moved upon the gradient scale of light expression,
you receive more information. You hear the voice of your soul
and the physical realm you had mastered has somehow shifted.
The boundaries of the reality you understood have faded. Still
present and almost instinctual are the default, patterned ways of
being that require no thought. It is exhausting as you examine

each thought that moves through your awareness. What we bring up today for your consideration is the possibility that if you feel old cues of discomfort and restlessness, you may be experiencing the edge between your physical reality and the truth known by your divine wisdom.

For example, the typical pattern for what would move you to action has often been fear based. Fear-based structures dictate, "Do this, or suffer the consequence." This is a negative message system that is survival based. Fear may still be present in areas you consider mundane and perhaps thought not applicable to restructure within your process of enlightenment. Each moment is a new opportunity for Love's light to shine. Again, beyond your doing, and living within your being, as you re-choose in moments where you notice fear, you open space for Love to emanate.

Choose Love

Allow fear to point you toward realigning with your divine expression. When you notice the discomfort of fear, allow it to point to the cause. Once the origin of the fear is seen, the door is open for new choices.
I choose to be informed by my highest divine expression.
As I align with my divine essence,
Love's brilliance shines upon All.
I return to the peace, joy,
Love, grace, and abundance that is mine everlasting.
And so it is.

As you stand in the light of your own divine essence, your thoughts, actions and being are imbued with Love. Fear is no longer the motivating factor. Love is now available as the messenger of action. As you allow Love to reign in all areas of your life, you open the door to Love's expression. Love is allowed to shine brilliantly through each area of your life. As you release the segmented compartmentalization that occurs with separation conscious-ness, you open the sash and fling open the door, allowing the vitality of Love to enter.

Day 281: Living Within Your Elevated Presence

Nothing is more worthy of you than you, walking in your elevated presence.

As you find ease in your elevated presence, you live a life that is worthy of your divine expression and that fulfills the original mandate of your soul.

What if you could live your life from the highest presence available to you? When you spend your Now moments within elevated presence you are informed by your I AM; the highest knowing of your soul.

From the space of your I AM, you are guided by possibility only available within the experience of the immaculate Now moment. Your personality's limitation is not present within I AM. Your soul characteristics are. Rather than fulfilling a mandate of personality informed by culture, you move in grace and light, emanating the radiance of your pure divine nature. The beauty of each moment is breathed in with appreciation for each and every rich sensory experience moving through your awareness.

You glide through your day with the ease made available in the absence of limitations. Arguments for or against particular topics disappear as you are present within a vast perspective, too large to focus on the right and wrong.

You are a stand for Love, you are a stand for the highest expression of Love. You experience the grace, beauty, abundance, joy, and divine knowing that reflect the sacred in All. Your potent emanation of Love's light transforms. Through perfect alliance with Love's synchronicity, all turns out well for you. You are in alliance with Love's highest expression. Your creations are collaborations of the highest order with an effect locally, globally, galactically, and throughout the multiverse. The gift of you is not available through anyone else. Who you are and what you offer is a precious, honored, potent, and sacred contribution to All.

Consider the reality of Love's reach when it is applied to your life. What becomes available when the experience of resistance is no longer? What is possible when the voice of your soul is heard?

Day 282: Owning the New Expansive Reality

As if you were at one moment living in the tight confines of a very small apartment, and then moved to the middle of the wide-open plains, where no civilization has lived before you, such is the experience of connecting with your new expansive reality.

As your conscious awareness expands, the shift is reflected in your perceived reality. There is a sense of more space around you and a feeling of reorienting to the expanse. Your reality is in fact deeper, larger, clearer, and steeped in the Love and promise of potential realized. If you allow yourself to perceive your reality beyond the habit you are used to, you find depth in the mundane, beauty in the simple, and the profound in the rays of the sun.

Like a bird freed from her cage, your vista is wide open, with no barriers to the exploration of what is possible. You are held in the light and Love of the sacred. Everyday experiences become reflections of the range of divine expression you are capable of.

Take a deep breath, Beloved, and behold the faces of Love.

Day 283: Allowance in Light

As you expand your awareness consciously to include what resides in light, you employ new methods of assessment that align with the qualities available in that light realm.

Remember, everything holds frequency: you, and your thoughts, intentions, beliefs, creations, and even relationships. Every expression lies somewhere on the gradient scale of light expression. As you move more consciously into the finer frequencies that reside beyond form and into the ethereal, you access more of your multidimensional nature. As your experience of expanding awareness gains velocity, the rules of your environment shift.

You are moving beyond the limitations of your thinking. Rather than your brain trying to solve a problem or innovate, you are connecting with the divine light access you have always had. Once held under the cloak of unconsciousness, now your awareness of action in light is accessible. Movement in light is not always direct, such as, "I would like an apple, so I go to the kitchen fruit bowl." Now, when you look for clarity, or pose a question, or are in prayer, the direct correlation is not as linear. Rather than your brain's mechanisms needing to figure the process out, you may take a deep breath, move to a high frequency space, and wait. Allow the information to arise within you.

It is this allowing of information to move toward you that accesses your greatest expression. Your divine wisdom resides in the light of your being. Your divine essence speaks to you through new ways, not necessarily through the way you are used to learning, communicating, and understanding. As you allow the light of Love to approach you, recognize that you are employing your greatest expression. Your deepest wisdom will reach you as you learn where to look and activate your divine being.

Allow Inspiration

- *Ask a question of your I AM that is related to clarity with a topic.*
- *Sit for a moment, asking all parts of you to be present.*
- *Take three deep breaths.*
- *Visualize yourself sitting at the edge of a huge magnificent lake. Allow yourself to BE in the space of elevated expression, raising your frequency. Be still.*
- *Allow clarity to arise from the surface of the lake to meet you.*
- *Be patient and know that, once you ask, the answer will be delivered.*
- *Become aware of your surroundings, sensations, and thoughts. Notice color, texture, and the resonance around you and the resonant tone that is experienced internally. Your message is delivered in a variety of ways.*
- *The action of inspiration is different in quality from the thinking process you are used to. Become curious about your unique process of communication in light.*

Even if you feel you are not connecting while you are in meditation, remain elevated to the best of your ability. The answer will be delivered as you continue to release a perspective that holds limitations. Be open to see clarity as you move about your day.

With practice, you will begin to find that the way you receive inspiration is a process that has always been present with you. This is subtle and beyond the density of what you know of as your typical thought process.

The door opens for a new level of communication. And the heavens sing.

Day 284: Miraculous, Naturally

When you invite your highest expression into your conscious awareness, you find that your divine nature is who you are ... naturally. There is ease, clarity, joy, and freedom in the Now moment as the barrage of noise that dampens your soul's voice falls silent.

The natural aptitude you have for expansion of your conscious awareness cannot be overemphasized. With terms like "woo-woo" and "out there" you buy into the separation between who you are at your highest divine expression and the limitations of being a "mere mortal," with only moments of the miraculous. The miraculous in the latter scenario is inferred to be the extraordinary, beyond expectations and rarely occurring. We would ask you to shift your awareness and connection with your truth. The miraculous is your natural way of being. The struggle that is imposed by the limitations of the physical experience is not the brick wall that appears impenetrable. It is a door to more of you.

As you turn the facets of the diamond of your most authentic expression you see the range of your expression rather than limitations. The limitation is perception, a self-imposed barrier. As you accept and acknowledge you have the highest say in your life's creation, you connect with your divine expression.

Rather than saying, "Well, the day is almost over, thank goodness." We say, what would have to occur in the shifting of perspective that would allow a thought that engages each moment with all you've got? The potency, beauty, clarity, and potential held in this

Now immaculate moment is your birthright, not an accident. You may shift your perspective powerfully, in the blink of an eye.

We bring this up today to ask you to consider your moments from the perspective of choosing your miraculous presence and creating potently from that space. What happens when you BE the miraculous? We ask you to consider what occurs when you hold the stance of your I AM presence.

You are the miraculous, naturally.

Day 285: You Are the Artist of Your Life

In Service to Love is a pathway for you living your best life.
The life you came here to live. You are the artist of your life.
Our messages are designed as catalysts, that your own divine
inspiration may take flight.

We remind you to choose the highest frequency possible in your thoughts, actions, and being. Once you move beyond the perspective that dictates creating your life from external circumstances and projections, you connect with the realm of possibility that is ever present as your beacon.

As you connect with the eternal stream of creation, possibility, potential, and inspiration that never wanes, the colors of your life are brilliant as they reflect the vitality, depth, and soulful alliance you hold with your divine expression. Learning to speak the language of your soul is a process both familiar and new. With practice you will gain the mastery you seek. The flow of inspiration and opportunity for divine collaboration is eternal and evolving.

You will notice that the quality of your creations is richer as you align with the inspiration from your highest expression. It is through developing an adeptness with shifting your perspective and frequency that you master creating your life. The power of your choice is informed with the potency of your divine nature, elevating life itself.

We invite you to live the vibrancy of the palette's many hues.

DAY 286: RELIABLE RESPITE AND COUNSEL

Today's message serves to remind you of the ever-present divine counsel that is available. In times of need you are never alone. Our presence does not step in and fix the moment, but shines the light of Love more brilliantly so you may be called to your greatest Self. And then you will see.

Dearest Beloveds, as you move through your life within an environment of a changing consciousness, the experience may be one of chaos, and may be unsettling, as you reconfigure reality within the expansive framework of your enlightened Self. There are times, moments, or days, when you request the presence of divine connection and support. We are always present for you.

Understand there is often a reflexive contraction that naturally occurs in moments of need. When you ask for our support in the moment, we respond. We guide you to the calm of the present moment and hold space for your new revelation. Allow yourself to be lifted into your higher knowing. A sense of expansion and cohesion accompanies the action.

Available in the asking, in the blink of an eye we are shoulder to shoulder. If you choose, we may go and sit by a quiet river and have a conversation. You will notice our questions for you, as we do not step over the line of choosing for you. We hold inviolate the freedom and sovereignty of all. The same conviction follows our support and guidance in aligning you with what you already know from the infinite stores of your divine expression. We are in divine collaboration in those moments. We are not rescuing you; that implies an imbalance of power. We connect, we meet, eye to eye, peer to peer, divine to divine, and always In Service to Love.

Day 287: Clarity with Expanding Awareness

Moving into an ever-expanding state of awareness becomes an art in the process of enlightenment. In response, what is required is an ever-adjusting way of being and relationship with what you once thought you knew.

The solid signposts and touchstones assigned to physical reality are now more present in light and less in form. Your experience in form continues to be a barometer for inner movement. You will find new parts of your being will move to the forefront. For example, if you held a belief system, likely unspoken, that placed you in anything other than an empowered space, it will come to the surface to be addressed by your conscious awareness. Aspects of your beliefs of self-value and imposed limitations become incongruent with your ultimate truth. In every moment you have a choice to examine your beliefs. The choices are before you and show up in your thoughts, events, and perspective. Incongruencies will rise to the surface of your awareness as you reach more deeply into the fine frequencies of your realm of truth.

The eternal flame of your being is a constant force. As you choose to expand your awareness, you begin to include the vast consciousness that is held by your expression in light. When you engage the principle that you *are* Source in form, you begin to see that there are no barriers between the wisdom that is accessible while you are in form and what is available when you are in light.

The barriers, once perceived as impenetrable, have shifted as you enlist the wisdom and clarity of your I AM. You are omniscient. When your I AM Self informs choices in your life, you have access to your greatest wisdom, and therefore your sense of limitation evaporates. We bring into demonstration the process of scribing this body of work. The information herein was not available until your Scribe entertained the thought that she is Source in form and the perception of limitations was recalibrated. Your divine access is you owning the part of your expression that resides in light. Like an exquisite sculpture that is bound in wrapping. As the wrapping is gradually removed, the true beauty that has always been there is revealed.

Clarity in the process of expansion lies within the sensation of resonance and the subtle experience of "knowing." Rather than the linear experience of lower frequency problem solving, resonance and the correlating physical response will relay a truth from a perspective that is beyond words and reason.

DAY 288: THE GRADIENT SCALE OF BEING

We have utilized the concept of the gradient scale of light expression to demonstrate the process of expanding consciousness, transformation, and enlightenment. This concept refers to the capacity that is held as your truth in totality, the full scale of expression from density to I AM illumination. As you consciously move on the gradient scale of light expression you access the broader perspective of your I AM Self unhindered by the limitations of form, habit, and belief.

Today we turn the facet of expression slightly to reveal another gradient scale. That is the gradient scale of being. The gradient scale of *light* refers to the level of access to your own I AM that you have attained. The gradient scale of *being* identifies ways the light from your I AM Self manifests in your physical reality through your ability to transform consciously. Your human nature must release limitations previously held in beliefs, habits, and consciousness to allow the expansive nature of your own divinity to be present in a way that makes a difference; otherwise, your potential remains in light and is not moved to form.

In uncovering the vast truth of your divine potential, you see that you are not just moving in one direction, as your awareness now holds depth and expanse. As you reveal the wisdom and divine perspective available through your I AM Self, your choices are informed by who you BE consciously, as opposed to your habits and unconscious ways of being. We have introduced the term "learn to dance the ladder of frequency" as a way to demonstrate your ability to choose your own perspective from the broadening palette of your capacity. So, the gradient scale of being could look like moving from point A, to point J, point Z, point M, and point D. When you hold the capability of sliding on the gradient scale of being, there is no sense of boundaries as there was when the limitations of the physical realm held you in place. You are less attached to your default way of being, so you may sense at times a feeling of drifting. In those moments, know that you are completely empowered.

Empowered Because You Say So
Select your way of being during the day. For example:

Today I am unstoppable. I hold alignment with my divine essence with purpose, grace, and ease. I am informed by my highest expression. I choose to be joy, creativity, and union.

As you choose consciously who it is that you are being during the day, you will find that your declaration then becomes the charted course that illuminates connection with your divine nature.

There are worlds between realization and actualization. Actualization mobilizes the potential that lies within your divine design. Like watching a sports game and being on the field playing. Two completely different perspectives are available. What we speak of today is the shift in awareness that moves what you are realizing into action in your moments. This concept further forges your process of actualization.

Day 289: Actualization, a New Potent Perspective

As you engage the new reality that becomes available for you, there is a choice about how to be with the awareness. Inspiration, revelation, and magical moments of alignment raise your frequency beyond the density of form. You may stop at any point, enjoying the experience of more connection, more joy, more Love, and more knowing. Yet, if you stay in the space of realization you are still held within the confines of limitation, albeit a guilded cage. Like hiking with five suitcases, then you discover you may put one of them down and feel relief when you do. But the fact is, there are still four more suitcases you are holding. Your enjoyment of the hike can get even better. There are always choices. We bring this up today to create a distinction. Allowing the distinction between realization and actualization into your creative expression opens a new potent stance. This new stance is the platform for the more-to-come that is available. Your divine expression is so vast, there is always more. *You* are the treasure trove. The voyage to your enlightenment is challenging. This is not a passive process. You place those items into your backpack that bring ease to the terrain you will be encountering. Consider that your terrain is shifting.

Realization will lift you to the heights to see your brilliance. The experience of actualization puts the realization into form. This is the point where you see you may actually alter your reality by owning the vast divine expression of your true nature.

At many points of your journey have you not said, "Oh, I have found it! Eureka, this is the answer!" then you find that the velocity that propelled you to that spot of your journey is somehow dissipated? That is because the movement to the revelation became your end point, rather than a point of beauty along your path. As you contemplate the distinction of actualization as your ultimate goal, the next steps will be illuminated.

There comes a point in the expression of light that you are when you really do move beyond limitations. Rather than hearing of great adventures, you are the adventurer.

When realization is allowed space for expression, you move into the action of actualization.

The experience of realization, even without actualization, is one that improves quality of life, adding joy, ease, peace, Love, and a broad perspective. It is the action at the core of actualization that continues the velocity of expanding awareness.

Day 290: Engaging Your I AM

It is in the echoes of the past that the weight of limitation resides.

As you have moved along the gradient scale of light, the distortion in your field that is a reflection of the layer of limitation experienced in the physical has been illuminated. You rise above the limitations of previous expression as you hold the Now immaculate moment with a new adeptness.

Today we speak about the diminishing field of resistance that allows a new level of clarity in union with your I AM.

I AM unstoppable in my message of Love.
I AM sourced by my divine essence.
I AM the miraculous.

Do you feel a new potency in these declarations? Do you feel the direct connection and amplified expression that is present? Earlier within *In Service to Love*, we utilized declarations as a way to center, align and move above the clutter and cloud of distortion. Now your perspective is expanded and your alignment with your center is clearer. You are informed by your I AM.

The connection with your I AM is eternal. Nothing has changed within the truth. What has shifted is your perspective. You are no longer swayed by the clouds of distortion within lower frequencies, nor are you limited by the perspective and boundaries indelibly placed by belief systems. Previously, a declaration of empowerment is most likely met with an internal dialogue that counteracts the action of the declaration. An internal dialogue within limitation would go something like this: "I am empowered in every area of my life. Then the internal voice reacts, "Not so much in my relationship though and definitely not in my relationship with money, but I would like it to be." Can you feel how a declaration made earlier in your process of expansion could have to go head-to-head with a field of limitation? At this point however, the declaration engages your I AM. There is a new quality that resonates truth. Your statements of I AM now hold a level of clarity, specificity, and potency.

Made within the Now immaculate moment, your declarations of I AM are allowed freedom to create powerfully. In the absence of distortion, your creations move swiftly. The consistent and persistent increase in your light expression contributes to your clarity. As clear water is added to a bucket of muddy water, gradually the whole bucket reaches a new level of clarity.

Sit with your declarations, allow them to move you. Feel yourself pulled into the high frequency of your I AM and allow that to inform you. No longer arguing with the limitations of the past, you are present within your Now moment and create powerfully, as only you can.

We greet you in the light of Love's eternal blessings.

Day 291: The No-Thing of It All

As you develop an adeptness at reaching beyond the limitations of your human nature to your exquisite divine nature, you access the space of no-thing. It is only within this rich environment of no-thing that the full realm of possibility is available.

When you still your listening beyond the din of the external world, your awareness is finely tuned, allowing you to hear your I AM Self with a new acuity. It is not as though this is a level of fine-tuned awareness that you must maintain all the time. However, once you develop the sensitivity for your own soul's voice, you will find you naturally seek your own counsel. Your center point of I AM is the connection with All, where there are no barriers.

The space of your I AM holds potential. It is within the immaculate Now that your potential is held as possibility. When you hold the high frequency space of the I AM, you connect with the potential within your divine design. As you sit within the rarefied space of you, your I AM directs creative charge, unhindered, to what is declared. Your I AM is generative, acting upon your choice and declaration. There is no staying still for your I AM. Your ability to hear and sense the multidimensional communication of your essence increases the more time you spend within the high frequency space of immaculate presence. Meaning you are fully present in the moment, unburdened by the weight of assessment, and available to hear what else is available.

As you commune with your I AM presence, you are experiencing the boundless expression of your truth. Beyond your declarations of creation, your I AM Self infuses every fractal of light that you have the capacity to hold. With fewer limitations, less resistance is present, allowing the messaging between your physical reality and the truth of your I AM to gain clarity, cohesion, and alignment.

As you Be the space of your I AM, you are present within the vast expanse of no-thing and All. From your increasing light presence, you invite alignment with your highest expression. Your high frequency moments catalyze potential into form. In the absence of limitation, your creations move swiftly.

As you engage your I AM, the potential you hold is not what you have experienced before. As you reach into the light of your being, possibility abounds. Allow your mind to move to the perspective of your own wholeness as the space from which you create your declarations. Know that you are accessing the golden elixir of Love's creation.

DAY 292: POINT OF CREATION FROM A NEW PERSPECTIVE

When you engage your I AM presence you are within a space of potential; a blank canvas with all the materials you would ever need to create from your highest expression. This level of creation is distinct from creation that occurs in every moment of your day. When you are going through your day you move through a myriad of states. From unconscious, uninterested, neutral, emotionally charged, fulfilled, joy filled, etc. Typically, it is not until an event or a thought triggers checking in that you search internally for your still center that supplies you with ease and balance. Therefore, your creations occupy a myriad of frequencies. You may look around you and see some that are not in alignment with your highest expression and some that are, and some that are neutral. Not everything needs to hold a high frequency, as your soul's evolutionary process is expressed through a myriad of conditions. What you bring to the table when you choose to create on purpose is a confluence of beliefs that would make that possible. As you believe beyond limitation you create beyond limitation. The frequency you hold while you create is a match for the frequency of the creation. So what could be possible when you hold the sacred space of I AM?

As the creation process is ever expressing, you are advancing along the gradient scale of light. What becomes possible when you are adept at holding high frequency space of your I AM presence

is the high frequency quality of your creations. In the enlightenment process, the voice of your soul is heard with increasing clarity. This is the space where your presence creates potently. As you
are aligned within your I AM presence, your expression crosses the
boundaries of limitation and you reflect your wholeness.

From our perspective the gift of your discovery of you is beyond
description. As you are all of your divine expression in each Now
immaculate moment, you transform creation beyond your knowing
of it. The levels of light you access are fueled by your soul's mission
of Love.

How great is that!

DAY 293: BEYOND THE CLOUDS

Your life has brought you to this Now moment. It takes something to live on the edge of what you have always known and beyond what is seen by most. Are you experiencing the excitement and vitality of your discoveries in light?

It is natural for collective consciousness to have tremendous influence on your expectations. When you grow up with the pressure of the collective consciousness, a dulling occurs as the clouds of limitation surround you and you no longer think you can fly. Today, we invite the return of the miraculous back into your experience. The miraculous holds the blank slate of no-thing and All, where you may be lifted beyond the clouds of illusion to where imagination and alignment with your divine nature soars.

As you contemplate your personal process of expansion you may ignite the mystery of the miraculous. It is natural in this process to interpret exquisite moments as normal so they may fit within boundaries of limitation. Today we invite expansion to the next level that has you reconnect with the miraculous that entertains possibility.

Increase the amplification of your signature energy as you choose. Allow your being to fill the room, your neighborhood, the city you live in, your country, all countries, the blue earth star herself. As you step back and see from the space of infinite being, miracles are as natural as breathing.

Breathe in the light of the miraculous.

Day 294: Connection, Communication, and Collaboration in Light

As you access more of the light that is yours, you reach the capacity of conscious connection with beings of light in light, beyond fleeting profound moments. Your connection in light is another aspect of your multidimensional and expansive truth.

As you are navigating your day it is possible to adjust your frequency to be compatible not only with the highest expression of you, but with All. So far, our conversations have been centered on your conscious connection with your highest expression, your I AM presence as an inner dialogue of sorts. Absent of limitations you hear the voice of your soul and allow that experience to inform your days.

Since there is no separation and All is connected, you may consciously connect with the Masters of light in light such as those present within this divine collaboration. The Masters we speak of are those that are at the source of this work with the highest expression of Love: Jeshua, Archangel Gabriel, Archangel Michael, Melchizadek, Buddha, Mary Magdalene, and the many more who constitute the matrix of *In Service to Love*. You may start with them.

Connection

- *Sit down and relax.*
- *Declare all parts of you to be fully present by saying out loud or silently:*
  I bring all parts of me present here and now.
  I bring all parts of me present here and now.
  I bring all parts of me present here and now.
- *Then, take three deep breaths.*
- *Feel yourself walking to your divine center.*
- *Gently move to your heart, allowing a centering and aligning to occur.*
- *Move to the space where your signature energy may be adjusted and expanded. Your signature energy is the energetic essence or fingerprint that is only yours. There is only one of you in all of creation. Your signature energy identifies you as you. You may expand, or turn up the volume of your signature as you claim your wholeness.*
- *Notice the experience of peace as it moves through every cell of your being. Allow the wave of peace occurring within the Now moment to release all tension in your body.*
- *In appreciation and in Love, request the presence of a Master of light in light that is most appropriate for you at this moment. You may also have a specific request, such as the presence of Jeshua, or St. Germain, or Archangel Gabriel, or Buddha. You may also notice the presence of your own Council of Light.*
- *Be with them. Feel their energetic signature. Communicate your intention for developing a conscious form of communication. Connect. Communicate. Then the possibility of collaboration may be communicated, if that is something that resonates with you.*
- *Be present. Be still. Listen to hear something new.*
- *When you are ready, return to your physical space and the appropriate frequency range for your day.*

You will feel a sense of well-being, peace, and the clear presence of Love. All this and more becomes available as you integrate the light that is your essential Self into your awareness.

We hold you in reverence, in Love and in peace. We delight in every step of the discovery of your mastery. Eye to eye, peer to peer, and divine to divine.

And so it is.

Day 295: Calling Upon Your Essence

Your I AM is ever present. Not dependent upon form, your essence resides as
your highest, most exalted expression.

In Service to Love places upon the altar for your consideration the possibility of living your physical experience from the perspective of your I AM. The perspective available from the I AM presence brings clarity, healing, and the experience of wholeness of All. Beyond the limitations of personality, your divine essence speaks into the world with a voice that transforms as it holds the essential note of Love.

Consider that greater clarity in every instance is always available. As you continue to drop the limitations in favor of a broader perspective, you access more of the light that is fundamentally you. The opportunity for raising your perspective is possible infinitely. The vanishing point of perspectives that are available for you is held at the I AM expression. It is your divine essence that holds the perspective of All, wholeness, and unity consciousness.

As you visualize a pyramid shape with the point at the top and wide at the bottom, consider that the highest amount of distraction and limitation is represented at the bottom part of the pyramid where collective consciousness resides. As you raise your frequency and shift your perspective to a higher viewpoint, your environment holds fewer and fewer limitations and distractions. In other words, as you raise your perspective, ultimately you reach your I AM expression and the presence of limitation is not a consideration. You experience Self as part of the whole, and the whole is Love. Love is All.

Calling upon your essence is the act of shifting your perspective beyond limitations to align to the greatest extent possible with your I AM expression. Remember, this is an uncovering of what-is as you continue to lean into the realm of the unknown, no longer informed by your past or expectations. In demonstration, imagine a light switch on the wall. The room remains dark, with obstacles unseen, until you switch on the light and the perspective shifts as more information and context is provided. The limitations of physical experience are present in the absence of the light of your I AM knowing. When you align with your highest expression you add light, perspective, depth, and a broader interpretation of truth. The arguing, debating, convincing of right and wrong are moot.

It is the values of light and dark that make up the texture of reality. Navigating the terrain of light and dark is the voyage of the soul in form. When you reach the point in your expression where you yearn for the more that is present beyond the seen reality, you reach deeper, beyond limitation, guided by the beacon of your soul.

A voyage worth taking. The treasure has been yours all along.

DAY 296: ABOVE THE FRAY

The divine essence of you seeks expression.

The option always exists to take the path of seeming least resistance and fall back into the habit and comfort of normalcy by blending in. As you continue your process of expanding awareness you will find that ways of being that used to work are not as comfortable anymore. There is a sense of unrest or lack of flow when you choose a version of reality that does not measure up to what you know of yourself. Today we shine the light so you may see the elevated experience above the fray of so-called normal living, where the voice of your soul may be heard. From there your days are infused with the vitality, joy, enthusiasm, peace, and beauty that is available always.

We get that the process of expanding awareness may feel exhausting at times as you continue to push against the tide of popular thought. We would like to reveal today another way you may move above the fray and experience your day from your most exalted perspective. We have discussed many methods of shifting awareness, such as increasing your frequency, increasing your signature energy, and adding light to your awareness in the moment. What follows is another method.

Refocus

If you notice you are experiencing a frequency, thought, or emotional state not in alignment with your truth, you may change the channel.

If you need to solve a problem, know you may shift your perspective by raising your frequency and moving your awareness to where the solution resides. Shift the experience by shifting your focus. (It sounds simple.) By choosing to shift your focus you are utilizing your expanded awareness to create. The act of choosing recognizes that you hold a broad range of expressions.

Shift your focus away from what you were doing. You may literally change the station of music. Stop what you are doing and focus on something different. Turn a new direction either literally or figuratively. Allow a point in nature to capture your attention; allow yourself to see the words you are reading with new eyes.

When you turn the page of your attention, you let go of the "flat" experience you find yourself in and see newly. This is practice in adjusting to your multidimensionality on purpose.

With the intention of releasing what you are doing, choose to refocus within the present moment. If you feel yourself within a whirlwind of thought, worry, or concern, you have most likely stepped away from the Now. Visualize yourself walking back to your own center. As with the outer rainbands of a hurricane, chaos abounds. As you walk to your center, you increasingly experience stillness and the reduction of static.

Discover your own creative ways to realign with your highest expression. Stop all thought and refocus to the moment. Allow the multidimensionality of your essence to speak to you. Your Scribe visualizes a beam of golden white light radiating from the heavens. If she feels out of alignment at times, she will literally take a step or two to one direction or another to be standing within the light of the beam that is within alignment with her I AM connection.

This is an experience that wipes the slate clean, allowing a more expanded awareness to be present.

You are at choice always to create an environment that supports your well-being. Beyond the external circumstance, you may hold the perspective of your I AM. Love, unhindered, knows no bounds.

DAY 297: THE LEGACY OF LOVE

The legacy of Love is wholeness;
A return to your authentic nature with nothing added and
nothing taken away.

Where one has opened to their true nature and expressed from the I AM presence, that space is forever imprinted with the signature of Love. When you visit sites that are holy, you feel the presence of Love and you feel the legacy of Love. Love is the sacred space that holds the miracle of transformation.

The space of Love's light not only transforms the environment, it transforms the present moment. Beyond the limits of time and space, ancient sacred sites still hold the reverberation of Love. As you express from your exalted I AM presence, your footsteps are illuminated beyond the physical realm.

You leave a trail of Love that conspires to transform. You are Love's greatest legacy and in turn advance the expression of Love.

As Love, you BE the answer to all questions. Bringing your light unbridled to the moments of your life is your answer to all.

You already hold all you need to play the symphony of your life full-on, at your highest, most authentic note.

DAY 298: THE THRESHOLD OF LIGHT

In Service to Love is intended to serve as a bridge between your human nature and your divine nature, where you experience your wholeness. There are many practices that temporarily relieve the pressures of the physical experience. Consider that managing your physical life is only one piece of the puzzle. As you peer beyond the fence of managing your life, do you see where you allow your essential Self expression in only limited circumstances? Do you see that your most essential Self is available always and lends a new perspective, grace, wisdom, joy, peace, innovative capacity, and comfort to all parts of your life?

As you are now inner-referenced, living from the inside-out, you develop the mental discipline and practices that support alignment with your own divine nature. Practices may be used for more than to release steam from the onslaught of your day and instead may be utilized to support your expression of wholeness. Do you see the subtle shift here? Your reach into the light expression of you, by your intention, continues. As you move within the light expression of your Self, the cues become more subtle, requiring a whole new level of scrutiny. Imagine being at a crowded and noisy mall. Then someone says, "Do you hear the fan?" What occurs is an immediate filtering of background static so your hearing may fine-tune to seek the fan. The same principle applies to your inner journey. This is not an experience of enlightenment in which you are anointed in one magical moment. This is your gradual and magical journey to your essential Self, where you learn to see the subtleties that communicate who you have always been.

Today marks another threshold of light to be crossed. The imagery is akin to the natural evolutionary process of growing up. As with leaving home for college, you already have everything you need to be successful in your next endeavors, yet to be revealed. Living beyond the curtain of illusion becomes a natural way of being now.

There are many pivotal moments in life that when experienced alter the course of what is to come. The potency held in the Now moment is met face-to-face with clarity and the knowing of your own truth. Once experienced, there is no backing out, because once you have seen the beauty and experienced the resonance and majesty of truth, it is a freedom that is transforming. The shackles of illusion are released.

And who does one Be when met with the miraculous?

DAY 299: THE DIVINE IN ACTION

The reality that is available through accessing more of the light of your divine nature is nothing less than a paradigm shift. As the lotus rises above the muddy riverbed to meet the magnificence of full actualization, you rise above the density of collective consciousness to BE your greatest expression. As you are sourced by the light of your divine nature, you reflect the beauty of your essential Self.

Adding the fine frequency of your divine nature to your conscious experience alters your perspective. Like a diamond whose beauty is revealed through the process of faceting and polishing, you now possess crystalline clarity. As you emanate from your highest expression, you are aligned with your I AM presence. You notice previous perceptions of limitation fall away, revealing your divine nature now unencumbered. You have developed keen awareness of your presence within the Now immaculate moment, the starting line for creation.

You hold an intention for this lifetime. In the absence of limitation, your soul's voice is available with new clarity and resonance. The field of possibility awaits your direction.

Allow your divine awareness space to express itself. Hold more of your moments within the immaculate Now. Align with your highest expression. Choose to no longer linger at the levels of consciousness that house your limitations. You have the ability to shift your frequency and rise above the constraints of thought and belief.

What is it really like to claim your own wholeness? We wait patiently for you to find out.

Day 300: Beyond Your Wildest Dreams; Creating from a New Stance

In the ups and downs of life, developing conscious connection with your divine essence is a game changer. The ability to rise above the limitations of physical experience is the action of the adept. You have moved beyond the reach of the influence of others now and find that the game of transformation is played on an internal field, not outside you. The reality that now becomes available is at times hard to believe. We suggest you continue moving beyond the mists of unconscious thought to view the ever-expanding perspective that is available.

The life of the adept does not mean that there are not difficult topics or moments. The adept recognizes the source of each perspective and weighs them appropriately, choosing from a space of resonance. It is in difficult times that the actions of the past are dropped, and the space opens for creating from a new higher expression. This is the feet-on-the-ground part of enlightenment. In the experience of enlightenment, your life is directed by the light of your inner resonance. Through your inner light of clarity, you may weather any storm. Beyond the challenges of circumstance and expectations, your path is lit with a new source of knowing.

As you are guided by your divine nature, a new higher frequency space is accessed. Resulting creations made from this exalted space reflect the magnitude of your own divine essence, catalyzing possibility into form. As you claim your wholeness, trust in the light of your wisdom that holds your greatest vision.

Continue to meet the Now immaculate moment fully. You've got this! We uphold our vow of guidance and support, and are eternally in service to Love.

DAY 301: FREEDOM FROM CONSTRAINT

When you live your moments from the perspective available through your divine nature, you naturally see beyond the curtain of constraint. What magical spell is this? It is the truth of you.

Consider the profound spiritual experiences you have had in your life. Was there ever a sense of limitation when you were in the moment with that experience? If you feel a sense of limitation or constraint, where is it coming from? There is a point of view that is a sticking point. The point of view itself is the constraint. When you find your way through the sense of judging your moments, you will find release of the constraints that have you held in bondage. And a new paradigm of your expression is available.

Pivotal in finding your way through restricting points of view is taking the stance of your full light expression. Imagine the you that becomes available after you transition out of this life. The space of no barriers. That is the space of knowing that is available for you at this moment. Restrictions and limitations become the beacons pointing to new discovery rather than barriers to the experience of your enlightenment. As you hold your intention and point of view aligned with your I AM Self, limitations dissolve and clarity becomes available. In contrast, if you choose a perspective that holds limitation, you will find, by law, a range of answers that hold a similar frequency to the concern.

The full-on expression of your divine nature is a process of
least resistance.
Enlightenment uncovers what gets in the way of living from
your wholeness.

A rose in the spring is pulled toward full manifestation of divine design with the summer ever beckoning. Even in the winter, the respite prepares for the experience of full manifestation. The rose does not stop at the expression of winter's dormancy, or spring's seedling or bud. The divine evolutionary spiral forever supports the full manifestation, according to the divine design. As you choose to look toward your divine nature as a reference point, you will see how effortlessly you are pulled toward your highest expression. In the process, the perception of limitation is released, and you experience the freedom of your wholeness.

The lotus blossom has long been symbolizing the process of enlightenment. With roots buried deep into the river's mud, the long stem reaches to the surface of the water, releasing the exquisite lotus bloom. Your finest expression lies beyond the experience of limitation. Your radiant beauty reflects the face of the divine.

So, we say, dearest Beloveds: Climb high upon the ladder of your divine expression. High above the clouds, the vast perspective of your I AM Self holds the answers to your questions. Your innate divine design holds a potential reality for you that is free of all constraints. More than a nice idea, this is a reality that becomes manifest as you hold your highest perspective and see with new clarity.

DAY 302: THE ARGUMENT FOR SUCCESS

It is the mental component of enlightenment that proves to be the most challenging. Through the conditioning process of physical life, you have learned to hold the mores and values of the collective consciousness. The path of enlightenment is finding your way through the entanglement of both mental and emotional weight.

You hold a myriad of values regarding how to craft your best life. You have views about your family, your work, your leisure time, your well-being, and your place within the physical experience in comparison to others. You have specific measures for success in each area of your life. And although there have been many successes, why is it that your highest expression has yet to be fulfilled?

We speak today about a new perspective relative to success. You and the majority of people you know assess their success as things they want and what they do. We suggest, as you align with your highest expression in light, that it is the external measures of success that shift. Success from the perspective of enlightenment is addressed through who you BE, not what you DO. And, most interestingly, it is through your divine expression that your greatest wealth may be accessed. As you Be the divine expression that is you, in the same way all the limitations become moot, so too do your heart's greatest desires now become possible. This is the experience of wholeness. Rather than choosing heads or tails in a coin toss, you hold the whole coin in your hand, and choosing becomes moot. You as Source in form already hold the potential and ability to fulfill all that you intended for this lifetime. As you live your life from the rarefied experience of I AM, you navigate success beyond your wildest imaginings.

Success is the fulfillment of your soul's mission. As you BE all you are, the limitations are not something to overcome, they just aren't a consideration. Yes, at the edge of the revolution of Love, bringing enlightenment to the areas you don't normally assign enlightenment status may feel like a stretch. As you consider the possibility of realigning your thoughts of success, you also bring your life's experience into a condition of wholeness. When you compartmentalize your life, you hold the space of separation. Everyday enlightenment. What would that be like?

Align with your highest expression in all. Realign your thoughts of success with the ability to access your divine nature. Who you are already is unlimited. The work you choose is a canvas to create from your essential Self. It doesn't get any better than that!

DAY 303: MOMENTS

Navigating moments of turmoil, confusion, and a changing collective global consciousness may leave you swirling in disbelief. The dizzying ricochet action of separation consciousness fighting for its existence is a challenge to live within. When you watch TV or read the news, move into a space of conscious awareness by stepping back and observing the dynamic. Rather than contributing to the right and the wrong, notice the divine in the process of choosing Love.

It is in the most dramatic moments of transformation around you that the veracity of your own inner journey is challenged. Remember this is the time you have prepared for. Have you noticed the moments of separation within your own life coming into view again? Choose clarity. Once an issue has you gripped, choose to see something new. Notice you are in reaction and make a new choice for how to BE within that argument. Wait for the reaction to clear, trusting that you can rise above the clouds, remembering the sun surely shines for you. The sun shines for All.

If you are looking for a helping hand, look back into the writings of *In Service to Love*. Notice which topic calls you. Practice raising your frequency, so that you may feel your own resonance more clearly. Your choosing is powerful. As you choose clarity, you will notice that the time you spend in a whirlwind of reaction will lessen. Trust that you will find your footing and see clearly again. As the collective consciousness searches for the return to Love, you too yield to the light of truth, revealing the areas that were forgotten within the darkness. All parts of you hold Love, nothing held back. From that perspective, do you see the gift of the experience of disruption?

Even in the moments of your process when you may not feel you are at your best, your truth never changes. You are Source in form. Every moment you spend through your endeavor to be enlightened is a sacred contribution to All.

Day 304: The Sacred Gift of Your Life

The blessing of life is understood and experienced when a new child enters the world of form. They are naturally imbued with the divine essence they came from. The divine is seen in nature, in the skies, in the mystery that abounds from the perspective of humanity. It is easy to feel small in comparison to the magnitude of creation's expression.

Do you view your life with the magic, the wonder, and the infinite possibility you assign to the newborn? Allow the expression of the sacred to imbue all parts of your life. Even the areas you may have placed in the category of "I can't transform that!" Place upon the altar of your being all that obscures your view of your own magnificence. Living from the profound is your destiny.

"Why then, Dear God, is life so hard? Why do I experience hardship and pain?" It is in the moments of most need that you have the opportunity to bring all of you to bear. Why would you reach for your highest expression if you have no need? It is the challenge of life you came here for. It is the difficult times, and the bad days, that forge the mettle of your being. Scour your inner landscape for what had not been seen previously. Your intention uncovers new perspectives that escort your potential to reality.

Beloved, you are the gift. It is in reverence and Love that we greet you. We celebrate and acknowledge the gift of you. Your forehead is anointed the blessing of sight, so that you too may see your reflection. We are awestruck as we behold your truth.

DAY 305: THE SOFT FOCUS OF LOVE

When you immerse yourself in the depths of your truth, your relationship with everything shifts. The detail of disagreements, disappointment, and self-judgment fades. Like a dressing placed on a wound, your own truth brings care and healing from the gashes created by life's hard edges.

What becomes available in the process of enlightenment is an aligning with your internal source of Love, creativity, and potential brought into form. As the frenetic actions of externally informed living slow to a halt, the new source of fuel becomes the light of your essential Self. The voice within your divine essence knows what you are capable of and gently invites you to fulfill your highest expression in all things. As when you learn a new language, the way life has been in the past no longer is large enough or potent enough to fulfill the vision you now hold. With the baggage of the illusion now behind you, your path is elevated to the realms of light you occupy naturally. The shallow experience of life as you knew it no longer holds your attention. You face the light of your soul's voice. You follow your divine guidance as the GPS for your Now moments.

Love brings compassion into presence. The compassion is first for you. The time spent on self-judgment contributed to the clouds of illusion that seemed unsurpassable. When you look through the lens of separation, you can't see the compassion you deny yourself, or the Love you may not receive.

When you finally see what has always been, you turn and face the light of your greatest expression. What had once seemed insurmountable is no longer even relevant.

The compassion next is available for All. From the perspective of I AM, you see the divine design in what has seemed like chaos. Rather than being pulled into the argument, you hold firm to your stance of Love as a presence on the planet. The expression of your vision becomes what you have always looked for and was in plain sight all along.

Love has always held you in embrace. Now as you see the larger picture, Love may be received and is expressed through your divine truth.

DAY 306: BEING CONSCIOUS OF EVOLUTION

Evolution is the expanding creation of the divine, in discovery and expression of the I AM Self. As you face the ever-changing landscape of your soul's journey to enlightenment, you contribute to the same process for All. Since All is connected, it may be no other way. As the propensity for the conscious presence of Love increases, you contribute at the leading edge of enlightenment for everyone. In the same way those in your lineage have contributed to you, you are a contribution Now to the evolutionary action of Love.

You are forging new pathways of thought and being. At one point the tide of consciousness will shift toward the highest expression of Love.

You contribute to the expanding awareness of All. Rather than holding firm to the way life has always been, you move to the forefront urged on by your inner compass. You have always known there is more. You came here to be a contribution. We would go so far as to say that if you are reading these words, you came here with a clear mission.

You hold a sacred vow. You may feel the presence of that within your inner knowing. Your vow is unique to you, yet your contribution is one spectacular note in the symphony of evolutionary discovery. You have chosen to join your voice in the choirs of the heavens. You have chosen to be heard above the din of unconsciousness.

You see the pain of those who have forgotten Love's promise for freedom. You hold on firmly to the demand for the exalted experience made manifest for All.

You live within the exalted halls of Love's finest leaders.

DAY 307: THE VIOLET FLAME

Your eternal presence in light contributes to your physical experience. As the mists of illusion are lifted, your expansive presence in light alters the way you view your reality. Rather than reaching deeply within the light from the perspective of physical expression, what begins to occur is that the light becomes your frame of reference. You have shifted your frame of reference beyond physical presence to consciously access your I AM.

As when shifting from coal to solar power, you now access a new energy source. The experience includes everything possible within the reality you are familiar with, and in addition, holds a higher frequency range of expression that is free of the burdens of physical limitation. As you release the restrictions of the physical experience, you hold the light of your essential Self. You are no longer cloaked in the vestiges of the past. You hold the expansive space of potential realized. Now what?

You hold the tools consciously to create at your highest expression upon the canvas of your life, unhindered by the din and chaos of the external world. You have always had a direct line to Source. At one time you considered this impossible, but prayed it was so. Now enlightenment is a pearl held within the palm of your hand.

Nothing has changed, and everything has changed. Do you feel your essential Self vibrate with the resonance of potential? The space has opened for you to learn more of your language in light. You now glean more information from your environment, from those you know and from Gaia herself. Your sensitivities are more finely tuned. Do you see how colors speak to you? Light holds information, consciousness, and frequency transmitted and received simultaneously. This new access is available as you choose. You can still choose the way life has always been, too. That never changes. That is free will.

If all restrictions you perceived were gone, what would you do? Who would you be? What would you create? How would you give your soul voice?

Today, we anoint you with the violet flame. The violet flame fuels the connection between your eternal divine essence in light and your experience in form. The violet flame envelops your heart, holding the bridge to your actualization. The threshold of realization is crossed. The space before you is nothing less than actualization.

And Now?

Sourced by the light of your divine essence, you are informed by your highest knowing. If you choose it to be so, we suggest that you consider meeting your divine team. We are with you at all moments. The Masters who resonate most and who move first to your thought is a good place to start.

Move to meditation. Take three deep breaths. Ask all parts of you to be present. Feel the vertical golden cylinder of light that enfolds you. Feel the violet flame at your heart. Ask your divine guidance to be present with you. Observe. Beyond your expectations, allow your knowing to expand. See the signature energy of your presence expand, sending out a clear signal of LOVE.

Allow your next step, your next creation, to come to you. You may have a sense of it at this point. Trust your vision will become clear at the right time. Connect with the voice of your soul. And what is there to be communicated at this moment? As you place yourself within the sacred space of your divine essence, wait. Creation occurs only in the Now immaculate moment. Allow your divine essence the space of no-thing and everything. See what shows up. In joy, and in Love, you will recognize your own voice.

Be still, and know that I AM God.

DAY 308: ALLOWING YOUR
EXPANSION

In the midst of your days, you get done what needs to be done, and you elevate your awareness, reaching beyond the mundane into the light of your essence. We speak today of the equal releasing and allowing that constantly takes place as you move into more of the ethereal light expression that is yours.

As you reach into your divine light expression you feel the frequency of your being increase. As always, there is another slight turn of the diamond that is you, exposing yet another facet. With movement of your awareness into finer light realms, consider *allowing* in equal measure.

As you move into the new space of your being, recognize that there is a natural, reactionary referencing or reflexive holding onto the known of your past. As you extend your awareness, there is a reflexive retraction. As you forge ever forward, shift your attention ever so slightly to the part of you that is giving way to the new expression, allowing the unknown to be present. Your soul strives for expression. Feel the part of you also that welcomes the new as a "finally we are here."

You hold many expressions. As you recognize, allow, and advocate for all of you, you give voice to all the components. It is with ease and grace for all your systems that the process of expanding awareness moves exquisitely in step with the divine beckoning of your being. Fueled by the light of Love as your Source, you are lifted on high. You begin to see All from the eyes of your I AM.

Beloved, we behold the grace of your countenance and reflect the brilliance of Love.

DAY 309: THE SEAL OF SEPARATION

Beloveds, the journey of enlightenment is not a journey that keeps beckoning and never allows you to arrive. The resonance of realization and the possibility of actualization move you forward with the force of your faith and the resonance of your footsteps. The end point of realization is when there are no more questions; for you cannot unknow what you now know.

The experience of realization is unique for each. As when you're on a grand voyage, and after a lot of time at sea being suspended between two realities, you finally come upon a light on the horizon. This is where we find ourselves. Each person reading these words will most likely say "perhaps others, but not me." A common experience. When you have not set foot upon the land, all is illusion, perhaps stoked by the vision held within the mists of an inner yearning. When you come face-to-face with the reality, you know a threshold has been crossed. The light of your knowing, and the warm embrace of Love, welcome you home. The paradigm shifts to the new discoveries available in expression of your wholeness. Possibility opens for collaboration with Masters who hold the same vision of Love, welcoming your unique contribution.

As you reach the shore of your essential truth, the next footsteps cross the threshold of the seal of separation. Consider the seal of separation as the barrier in place until you are ready and choose to move beyond the illusion of separation to the reality of your unlimited nature. What could be possible then? Beyond the rhetoric and guessing, your inner knowing recognizes truth. The result is the freedom of expression within the embrace of Love.

Your journey has been initiated by you, always. Your path is divinely supported and energetically charged, reflecting the dynamic multidimensional truth of your unique passage.

As a child is in the birth canal during the process of transitioning into form, the cervical tissues of the mother thin, allowing passage of the child to a new reality. The breaching of the seal of separation occurs as you reconnect with the light of your divine expression. What does that feel like? You are unstoppable in your mission of Love. As a rose is unstoppable in being the full exquisite expression of rose. You are more of you; nothing need be added, and nothing taken away. Your alignment in light is matched with your physical reality. You draw upon your knowing in light and bring that to bear in your life. You move in light with joy, freedom, and the knowing of Love. The increasing presence of divine light that has been your stepping stone is a contribution to your overall well-being mentally, emotionally, physically, and spiritually. You possess everything to fulfill the mission of your soul's perfect contribution.

We kneel, in reverence to you, Beloveds. To undertake the journey you are on requires courage and a sturdy constitution. You, as leaders in the revolution of Love, are Masters.

DAY 310: LET THE SUN SHINE

Your presence shines more brilliantly as you access the light of your divine nature. How could it do otherwise?

The result, however, is a shift in your reality. You have an immediate reaction to the thought of your reality shifting. Note that reaction. It is normal. For it is something that your identity considers a threat to the status quo of the presence of the illusion. Your identity is an argument for keeping life as it is. "Everything is just fine. Nothing needs to be changed. Well, maybe a few positive thoughts here and there, but nothing major," or something like that. However, the essential expression of you runs deep. The deep resonance from the voice of your soul speaks in a language beyond the physical experience. Your soul speaks beyond your understanding of it, deeply into the resonant field of your divine essence. It is for this that we shine light to clear the path for the footsteps you are at choice to take.

As you develop the conscious awareness of your process of enlightenment, you choose on purpose with clarity. Otherwise you know your default system of identity and past experience will prevail.

You will notice shifts in the perception of your reality as the light of your most authentic Self emanates ever greater. You hold a frequency that rings with the clarity of your soul's mission. The potency of your presence transforms your environment. Everything that is within the reach of your light of Love is elevated to a higher frequency. Love reigns as you allow the light of your essential Self to shine naturally.

Life is good.

DAY 311: LOVE'S ACTION OF WHOLENESS

In the light of Love all is restored to wholeness. As the light of the sun is a catalyst for the flower's budding in the spring, so too is the light of Love the catalyst for the expression of you toward manifestation of your divine design. The light of Love restores your wholeness always. When the weight of illusion within low frequency is lifted, the natural alignment with your divine nature is experienced without resistance.

A laser is efficient and precise as it reaches its target. When the beam of light is deflected, the specificity of the light's action is diffused. Meaning, as resistance is present in your beliefs and ways of thinking, the expression of your divine nature is not experienced at full potency. Unconscious beliefs and awareness residing in the past or the future deflect the full expression of the light of your divine essence.

When intention is held for wholeness, the light of your divine essence moves with clarity toward expression in your physical experience.

Love will always lead you toward your highest expression, toward freedom, toward peace, toward the manifestation of your essential Self. Understand that the goalposts continue to move. As you seek your highest expression made manifest in your physical life, your I AM continues to evolve. There is nothing that is stationary about you.

You are an eternal symphony in search of the next resonant note to be contributed as Love's gift to All.

DAY 312: ENTRAINING TO HIGHER CONSCIOUSNESS

All creation evolves. To this point we have been offering, for your consideration, empowered perspectives to be realized through your own resonant process. Not as told to you by us or told to you by another, but as realized through a deep knowing that is attained only through the resonance of your being. You have shifted your perspective away from the limiting expression that is the result of being informed by beliefs or by others outside yourself. This new shift in perspective allows you to develop more pathways to connect with your own divine wisdom. It is this process we support. The brilliance you already hold needs no improvement. It is our intention to support a shift in perspective that allows you to see for yourself the truth of you. We are at another pivotal point today in perspective.

You see the value now of your own connection. You are developing the remembering of your own language in light, your mother tongue. Innate and beyond the mind's ability to comprehend, you have been reaching more deeply into the light of your own divine truth, accessing the wisdom you have always held. Today we shift one more time to the consciousness that enfolds you. The consciousness of Love.

Located within the Now immaculate moment, elevate your perspective to feel the partnership with your I AM Self and the Masters who reside in light. This represents a new, more expansive perspective. Imagine a series of concentric circles. The internal circles represent a personality-focused consciousness. As you continue to expand your awareness you vibrate at higher frequencies as you gain an ever-broadening perspective. Your consciousness at each step enfolds the previous levels of consciousness, and you are elevated. As you move along the gradient scale of light expression, you align with the exquisite note of Love itself. When you take your seat at the table in your quest to BE-come, you begin to contribute consciously to the evolution of Love itself. Connected to All, you move in the beautiful dance of Love.

No matter which level of contribution you choose, know that every single step you take in the name of Love reverberates throughout creation. You are perfect, whole, and complete, whether you choose expansion of consciousness or not. We create a pathway for those who hear the yearning of their soul and choose to move beyond the edge of what they know.

Forever, you are Love. You are the Beloved.

DAY 313: THE ONE THING

One thing you may always count on is the eternal expression of
divine Love that you are.

In the realm of variables in your day-to-day living, most of you
search for the *next* thing. The distinction we make here is the
choice to look for the *next* thing or the *one* thing. As you hold before
you the next thing that catches your attention, your search is fueled
in part by a reorganization of what you have already known, influenced by what is in your external environment. A remix of sorts.
New and improved, most likely, but is it the "thing" you are really
looking for?

The one thing is fueled by your divine nature. As you look
toward your I AM Self for guidance, you access your highest knowing, informed beyond the restrictions of past and into the higher
expressions of frequency available within the field of your totality.
When you choose to search for the one thing, all the rest will lay
out in front of you as a progression of high frequency, inspiration, surprise, and delight, with resonance on a deep level. You
are always informed by your unlimited nature. Everything that
gets in your way, or that clouds the light of your essential truth,
will show up not as obstacles but as opportunities to move beyond
restrictions.

As you hold the perspective of aligning with the voice and
vision of your I AM Self, you are elevated naturally. You are present
within the Now immaculate moment, which is where your most

potent creation resides. You recognize resonance and allow resistance to be diminished as you allow and receive all that is yours. Your presence within the Now moment supports your movement into uncharted territory, where new discoveries are made. Each discovery rings with high resonant value.

As you search for the next thing, you receive just that. As you search for the one thing, you open untold possibility, and your soul sings.

Day 314: Shifting Perspective to Match the Your Access to a New Paradigm

The new paradigm you are within is only helpful to the extent that you realize you are in a new paradigm and employ the landmark perspectives that are commensurate with the paradigm. Consider that you now have access to a higher level of functioning, which is natural to you. Think of owning a car: Rather than having the car sit in the driveway, there are certain actions that are required to employ the new paradigm or experience of "car." You need the keys, and then you need to open the door. At that time, a whole new set of rules are in place for movement within the paradigm of car. There are rules and regulations, laws, and specific awareness around transportation. The result is an exponential increase in possibility.

Beyond shifting your awareness to engage this new paradigm, you must first employ a new set of actions that are commensurate with the new broader perspective you hold. Action in the past has probably looked like tactics, plans, management, and philosophies for how to master the physical realm.

Now, as your conscious awareness has expanded, doors to a new paradigm are open. Living on the edge of what you know and what you do not know becomes a conscious expression. When the doors to a new paradigm are open, there are perspectives to be explored that propel your awareness to an even greater extent. The point of view you have used up till now will not carry you into the new space. What if you are Source in form? What does this mean to you now that you have connected more deeply with your own divine nature? When you stand in the illumination of your own divine essence, you already have All. From the wisdom and vision available from the standpoint of your I AM Self, your declarations are potent. You have access to your multidimensional awareness and capacity.

Consider the subtle difference between creating from the limited perspective of wanting versus the expansive perspective of choosing. From the perspective of your I AM Self, you neither want nor need. You choose. You summon. You declare. As when you go to the cupboard to get a coffee cup, you choose with ease and with clarity. The background is always Love and appreciation for All.

As you engage your divine nature, there is a sense of being in concert with the universe. You are no longer alone. You feel communion with All and you access Love as the Source of creation.

Consider sitting with this a bit. Allow the difference in perspective to arise in your awareness. Take the reins in a new way and allow the brilliance of your light to create, informed by your I AM Self.

What a gift you are.

DAY 315: THE BLESSINGS OF LOVE

L ove holds many blessings. Love is nonjudgmental and does not discriminate. Love is ever present. Bring yourself to Love's doorstep to find the riches of your I AM Self. You may engage Love at every level of expression, from the most limited, illusion-filled spaces to the rarefied air of enlightenment, realization, actualization, and beyond. All you need to bring is you. In whatever space you are in, whatever mood, good day or not-so-good; reverent and resonant with the sacred or reveling in the joys of pure being.

In all cases you, dear One, are the one who chooses at which level you connect with Love's blessings. As you have entered into the collaboration of *In Service to Love*, there have been many access points into the space of Love's grace. In each and every case you are the one who chooses. Each step taken as you release who you are not has required something of you. The road to enlightenment holds many paths. You choose the path that resonates with your deepest knowing. As you release the shrouds of illusion, you see more easily the presence of Love in All.

If you choose the full enchilada of enlightenment, it is available for you. As you claim the light expression of your divine nature, there is a point at which you may not move beyond without actualizing your awareness. Consider moving your expanded awareness into action in your physical life. This is another point of adjusting perspective. It is natural to hold awareness internally. Consider that you came here for more. What this looks like is walking the talk. Really, what does it feel like to be Source in form? How does that change your day? How does that affect your actions, thoughts, feelings, and creations? The next space is one of fine-tuning your awareness and being informed increasingly by the light of your I AM Self. As you shift to living from the perspective of being inner referenced, you access vision and wisdom that is distinct from thinking. You experience more of you.

This is not the only pathway to enlightenment. It is a divine collaboration of Love designed to support your process of expanding awareness, revealing your exquisite brilliance so you may be the contribution you intended. Actualization is an experience of ultimate freedom. As you access your authentic nature, you have moved beyond the restraints of physical, mental, and emotional limitation to be informed by your divine knowing. You dance with the choreography of your soul's rhythm. This is not a test; this is a choice of your soul. You need not suffer through the "threshing floor" of Love. Love resides in wholeness. Love is a space of grace.

Wherever you choose to engage Love, Love is here to meet you. We, as Masters of Love in light, are always here to engage you at the level you choose. There is always more. You don't need to be at the end of the journey to receive Love's blessings. Love is here Now. And always will be.

DAY 316: THE EVOLUTION OF LOVE

L ove evolves. There is nothing within creation that remains static. As we speak of the process of expanding awareness, the end point of expanded awareness, enlightenment, realization, and actualization is evolving as well. As you are within your ever-enlightening process, your life may be expected to shift. The purpose of expanding awareness now is to create beyond the illusions of physical expression and create in your life, with the freedom, clarity and ability that is natural to you.

In short, your process of expanding awareness is intended to improve the quality of your life greatly. So, it follows that your life would change. As you take the reins in your life—meaning, you begin to create from a conscious perspective rather than one that is unconscious, lived by default or habit—your life will improve in all areas.

So what is getting in the way? If you are finding areas in your life that are not shifting as you would like them to, we ask you to consider directing the full force of your essential nature toward these areas. We are within the last 60 days of this particular iteration of *In Service to Love*, which contains 366 entries. So, it is reasonable to expect that areas of your life would shift to be in line with the divine nature you have been able to access.

And So It Is!

Choose an area of your life experience you would like to transform. Sit and be quiet; move into stillness and allow the topic that is ready for conscious expansion to inform you. Choose only one for now.

Sit with that topic; feel the scope of the topic as it is right now. Feel the weight of the energy you hold around it. Stay in the position of observing how you are with this topic. Rather than becoming the concern, observe it. Observation is a critical perspective shift.

Move to the perspective of your I AM Self. Feel the unimpeded light of your divine nature. Feel the vertical golden white light cylinder that is around you always. Within this high frequency space of light, feel the pull that is moving your expression always toward wholeness. Like a tractor beam, feel the light expression of you, pulling all of you toward wholeness.

Now bring the concern or issue you would like to transform into the beam of light that is also moving toward wholeness. As you move the concern into light, you will feel the weight of the topic dissipate.

Hold the space of freedom with this topic. What is getting in the way of transforming certain areas of your life into their highest expression is the weight of the past, the weight of expectations, and the weight of fear. As you add the light of Love around this topic, the weight will shift. Without moving toward your thinking skills, move your topic from the space of "weightedness" to the space of light.

Allow a new way of seeing this topic appear to you. If you were new to the planet and had no idea of the "meaning" of things, you would hold a neutral stance. Move yourself to a neutral stance with this topic and move the topic deeper into the light. What do you have to let go of around this topic in order for it to express in a higher frequency? Hold the higher frequency space until you feel complete. Is there a sense of greater ease?

Stay out of a fixing mode. If you could have fixed this before, you would have. Consider that your problem solving is not accessing the frequency that the solution to this issue resides within. So, shift your frequency awareness to the band of frequency that holds this topic in wholeness. Release the weight of the issue and allow it to rise into a new expression. Rather than jumping toward a solution, allow a new perspective to come to you. The new perspective will be informed by your highest expression. Allow it to work with you. As you do, you demonstrate your wholeness and your adept capabilities of shifting frequency range for specific purpose.

Notice the inspiration or new thoughts that move to you over the next days and weeks. Continue holding this topic in the high frequency space of light, in movement toward wholeness. Rather than react and hurry into action, we ask you to wait. Allow the new awareness to arise within. You haven't seen them before, but you will recognize them.

When you have clarity, your action will be natural, not something you do in order to fix. You will notice you will be in the moment. As you stay in the moment with your topic, the issues of the past will also fade. Allow the past to fade as you hold the magic of the moment.

DAY 317: PERFECTLY NATURAL

The process of enlightenment uncloaks your divine nature. It is not a space to be attained as much as it is a process of releasing yourself from who and what you are not. So, if most of your life has been conditioned with what you are not, then as you release all the perceived limitations, you experience wholeness.

You are designed to function perfectly. The communication from you in light to physical reality gets bogged down by the weight of the illusory definition you hold of yourself. We would say the most challenging concept in the process of enlightenment is you opening your definitions wide enough to see, feel, and be the divine. Before you really get the perspective that is available to you, you see yourself through the reflections of the divine. Gradually through the resonance that signals you are "getting warmer," you begin to stand in the light of your own truth, within the immaculate Now, and you see your divine truth clearly.

Your expanding consciousness brings to light what was hidden, and this is where the rocket of you takes flight. You no longer wear the blinders that limit your vision. You are unburdened and can get to the work you came here to do.

Begin to feel more comfortable in the unhindered space of your divine nature. As you have been going through the work of releasing, you are at a new beginning. You are Now present with you. Do you feel the lightness of being? The field of possibility vibrates around you.

Getting down to the bedrock of you is just the beginning. Now what? What is it that deserves your light and attention?

We are giddy with anticipation.

DAY 318: RELEASE OF COMPARTMENTALIZATION

When you incarnated into this lifetime, you chose to compartmentalize your physical experience so that you had the opportunity to move in the direction of your soul's highest interest. As you have evolved, the need for compartmentalization no longer meets your highest needs. If you are reading these words, the chances are high you have moved beyond the limiting experience of compartmentalizing your life and are ready for the freedom that is available within your wholeness.

Compartmentalization is a valuable tool to support the focus needed for specific areas of growth. If you came into this life unconscious and were exposed to the vast expression of you, it would be destabilizing and not supportive of your well-being. However, the tide has turned since you were born. Not only have you evolved, but the experience of your world and all creation has evolved. You are no longer held within the confines of separation consciousness. The journey to your wholeness is supported with the presence of unity consciousness. This timing is what you were banking on when you incarnated. You intended to move through the darkness into the light. You intended to be the contribution you know you could be at the vanquishing of separation consciousness. You are a leader in the revolution of Love.

With access to the knowing you possess in light, compartmentalization no longer fits you. Compartmentalization is confining and appeals to the limitations of personality. Within *In Service to Love*, the faceted expressions of you have turned, and turned, and turned, revealing the expanded awareness that is you authentically. As these shifts have been in resonance with your specific path, new realms have opened to you, and the defining experience of compartmentalizing your life just doesn't fit anymore. As you recognize the vestiges of compartmentalization in your life you have the opportunity to move beyond imposed limitations so you may shine brightly. Your wholeness is not expressed through conditions.

The way this appears in your day is in recognizing that the access to your wholeness is not conditional. You possess a broad spectrum of wisdom and depth of awareness. You have the capability of owning your full spectrum of expression and then choosing where it is used. This is different from the narrow viewpoint that is present with compartmentalization. As you bring All of you to bear in your life you are pulled forth by the divine expression of you into your finest potential, realized.

Continue to move in your day with the full freedom of your totality. Feel the wholeness of your expression as fully informed by your divine knowing. This is the ultimate in authenticity. Move ideas, thoughts, and situations to a higher frequency space to gain clarity. Allow the brilliance of your divine knowing to pull you forth into the greatest expression of you.

Expect joy, freedom, and peace. Expect Love. It is in Love that we greet you.

DAY 319: THE COHESIVE FORCE OF LOVE

Love is a creative force. You as an expression of Love are a Master creator. As dissonant and resonant notes of potential meet the creative force of Love, they begin to match the frequency of the highest creative intention. The resulting creation is brought about through the cohesive and organizing force of Love.

Consider that you, as a being of light, hold infinite possibilities within your field of light. What is it that organizes the creation into movement in your field of awareness? It is the cohesive qualities of Love. When you hold presence within the Now immaculate moment, in the still presence of I AM, of pure Love, the realm of potential around you awaits direction.

You have an ability to create within a variety of conditions. You may create from low frequency, resulting in creations that hold low frequency. You may create from the space of past experience, and those creations hold a recycled type of energy. You may create out of fear of the future, and those creations hold a vibratory calling card of fear, inviting separation and low frequency results. All spaces are platforms for creation. Although familiar, it is the lack of resonance that has these creations not sing within your being. As you get used to the disappointing "thud" of uninspired creations around you, the rare moments of profound experience feel like a much-needed lifeline to your thirsting soul.

We speak of the cohesive force of Love to remind you of the natural capabilities you already use to create from the space of the divine. You hold the ability and perspective now to be able to create from a high frequency that supports the mission of your I AM Self. There is no need to feel resigned to disappointment with the way you create in life. You now see what you could not before. As your intentions are in resonance with your soul's expression of wholeness, the details become moot. The greater vision is your main focus. You will find the manifestation that results from holding a high frequency focus will be in alignment with your intention beyond your ability to determine, calculate, or manage events. Your full potential awaits your direction. We ask you to move to your highest frequency space. Hold the greatest intention of your essential Self thus:

Access Love's Organizing Force

Move to the Now moment and hold the greatest vision, the all-out manifestation, of your soul's intention. Who you are is unstoppable in your wholeness.

> *I choose the manifestation of my highest expression, mentally, emotionally, physically, and spiritually.*
> *I choose my own wholeness made manifest.*
> *I choose Love.*

Allow inspiration to arise in your awareness. Hold the creation of your intention in full actualization. You are the conduit for moving the creation from light to form. You do so through your access to the light of the Love that you are. Within the high resonance of potential within the Now immaculate moment, your Love is potent. The banquet of Love's creation lies before you.

As you hold space within your full divine expression, your field of potential vibrates with possibility. What do you choose to create from your I AM presence?

Day 320: Enlightenment: The Pathway to Your Genius

The pathway to your genius is lit by the flame of your true nature.

As you have embarked on your journey of enlightenment, the restrictions and weight of what you are not have been lifted. Your own genius is revealed.

The actualization of your genius lies in potential, waiting for your collaboration. The collaboration we speak of is the embodiment of your own divine nature. Your reach into the light of your highest expression activates the potential that is yours.

There are areas of your genius you have yet to uncover, and still, the genius that is available in this Now moment is brilliant. Beyond the physical limitations, your divine collaboration is an expression of your wholeness. When your human nature aligns with your divine nature you access your multidimensional, divine capacity. In essence enlightenment is the embodiment of you. Rather than being bogged down by lower frequency endeavors, continue to look beyond information of the past to what seems to be just out of reach. It is the reaching into the unknown that propels you forward. With each new step within the Now immaculate moment, the light of your essential Self illuminates your path.

It begins with your faith in you. The results that are possible from your full presence in the Now moment may not be anticipated. As you raise your frequency and show up in the Now moment, propelled with the intention to be more of you, notice how your anticipation, curiosity, Love, and delight begin to shape the canvas upon which you create.

The joy of being in the Now moment is never really knowing what will happen next. The Now moment is the direct access to your divinity. Each moment holds new promise. Love must create. Love must evolve. As you hold strong to your intention to create from wholeness, allow each moment to inform you. Allow yourself to be surprised. If you already know what was going to happen, you are limiting your expression.

Shoot for the stars. Ah! There you are.

With Love and delight, we remain,

In Service to Love,

The Council of Light

DAY 321: TODAY

Today. Today is the day you have been waiting for. You are the One. You are the One you have been waiting for. The possibilities are endless. Today is the day you reach to the stars and you reach beyond what you have searched for before. Today you are guided and informed by your highest divine essence, your I AM Self. You see? You have never been separated from your divine essence. It is who you are. The clouds of illusion are all but gone for you. You have turned over each stone of your awareness, and the treasure you have always been looking for is the one looking.

Today is the day you release your hold on limitations encased within your humanity. Today, you add to the physical experience you are familiar with, an unknown elixir; the expanding elixir of Love. As you are within the Now moment, here on Gaia's sacred ground, you actualize your own sacredness of being. Within each pathway of enlightenment is a moment. The moment of, "Aha! I get it." The "it" for you to get is the sacred expression that is you, *really* allowing your brilliance to shine during your life. It means reaching beyond what you have done to be who you are. The limitations of your past are now contributions, not your definition.

Today, as the butterfly must emerge from the chrysalis, you, too, emerge from under the cloak of limitation into the light of your own divine truth.

Today, we, as Masters of light in light, serve you, in reflecting back to you your vast magnificent sacred essence. Love in action Now.

DAY 322: A NEW CADENCE

With the opening of and aligning with your divine nature, your capacity for light expression has expanded. This brings with it a new way of being. You are no longer informed only by your five senses. You are informed by the part of you that resides in light and that carries the uninhibited expression of your I AM Self.

As the light of your divine expression informs your thinking, you move beyond the functions of linear understanding. You will notice ideas coming to you in new ways, almost as if falling out of the clouds. "Wow! Where did that come from?" As your divine nature has more room within your conscious awareness, life will be informed to a greater extent by your soul's perspective. The information of your essential Self is both received and transmitted at the same time. Unlike thoughts that have a process, your movement in light is rapid and clear, as it is not met with resistance.

As you release your attachment to memory and the way things have been in the past, you are more able to hit the target of presence in the Now immaculate moment. The combination of presence in the moment and your highest light expression sets the stage to create at a high frequency. Without the emotional baggage of solving a problem, of needing or wanting, you move easily to a place of choosing and of summoning as you stretch into the light expression that has always been you. You will find the emotional attachments are often littered with baggage that may turn your creations into repetitions of past expressions. So stay clear of emotional baggage, with the ongoing practice of presence in the

Now moment. As you develop your mastery of the Now, the inspiration and direction of your light essence filters increasingly into life's moments. You will feel less burdened, lighter, and curiously unattached to your past.

You move now in light with ease. Your resonant tones of being are distinguished and allowed space to express your divine truth. You live your life on purpose and in alignment with your deepest soul's desires.

Welcome home. With great delight, we celebrate all of who you are: Love at its best.

DAY 323: ON PURPOSE

Even though you have expanded your capacity for spending moments in the light of your divine essence, have you noticed life still happens? What we place on the altar today is a way to be with those times, moments and days, when you feel off your center.

Your experience in the physical realm has events that don't stop because you now have a broader perspective on them. The gift now is your capacity for a broader awareness that allows you to look beyond the events that are in front of you to the larger picture. This broader perspective will limit a lot of your reactions; however, there will be times when you find yourself right smack in the center of reaction. And you look to get out of it. The natural inclination will be to stop your reaction and look for something that is not seen, or most likely to reach into your past for clues. Consider that the act of resisting reaction is a separation of it from you, and this in turn creates more resistance. If you can acknowledge that a part of you is needing clarification, you may move through with ease. Rather than react to your reaction, choose to be in the reaction on purpose.

When you allow the reaction to be a part of your totality, you will have access to your higher knowing that is limited when you are in resistance.

Allow. Notice. Be gentle.
What part of you needs a voice?

Rather than looking conveniently to problem solving, allow the emotional content to speak. When you are present for the voice of your concern, you hold the space of observer. You are no longer the problem, and no longer the reaction; you are accessing the highest perspective available. Give it some time. Notice how you are being with the reaction. As you access the space of observer you are fully present within the Now moment. You can more easily see how your participation in either the past or the future has influenced your reaction. The stance of observer allows the issue to move into the light of your knowing and into wholeness, where reaction is transformed.

As you begin to view physical reality as new every moment, you approach your day from the stance of observer. Your unconscious expectations are no longer guiding your creation. You allow space for your own inspiration and creative flow to move around you. The gift of reaction, difficult times, and challenging situations is in who they allow you to BE.

There is a silver lining present in each dark day. If you can be curious rather than reactionary, you will see the brilliance of your divine light expressing your wholeness.

DAY 324: THE LANGUAGE OF LOVE

As you reach into the light of your I AM Self, you encounter the
beingness of Love.
Love is amorphous, found in reflections of the divine.

The search for Love seems to run through your fingers and out of your cupped hands. A glint of light in your periphery, the innocent light in a child's eyes; the glint of knowing. The language of Love is a way you BE.

The experience of Love is behind, and at the core of, all you do. Who you Be is Love. When you allow yourself to yield to the gentle familiar beckoning of Love, you align with your stillness at the center of your being, within the Now immaculate moment. "How do I get there?" you ask. Be still, be still; wait to hear something new. Release the thoughts of your day, of your moment, of your thinking. Between the words, between the inhale and exhale, is the surrendered and potent language of Love. Your words are informed by the Love that you are. Your actions are informed more clearly by the Love that you are. You find those times where in the heat of the moment, you see that your presence is not at your center and you have lost the moment. Like holding a fine silken thread without breaking it. You finally see that as you simply hold your hand outstretched, rather than grabbing on, the thread shines and sparkles, revealing its mastery.

So it is with Love; as you go about your day, look deeper. Release what you know to reveal who you really are.

Love Knows Love

Practice sitting in the space of Love. Give yourself the gift of quiet moments. In those quiet moments hold the intention to connect with your essential Self. Release the layers of the façade. Release the layers of knowing. Release the layers of thinking. Like the stilled quiet that comes with a winter's snowfall, allow the edges of your day to soften. Come, dear One, to the present moment and meet therein. It is Love at its most potent expression. Release who you are not, so the true Love you Be may shine. Allow yourself to be embraced by the rapturous healing, and restorative experience of your truth. Allow the high frequency of Love to restore you. Allow the Love you are to recalibrate your physical expression. Allow Love's wisdom to infuse your being, activating the cellular wisdom that is innately yours. Love knows no limitations.

Bask in the light of Love's expression. Fall deeply, madly in Love with your divine nature. Like one perfect snowflake, you are One. You are unique, perfection, a sacred gift to All. Your reflection is seen in the sunrise, in the glittering night sky. Release the weight of your physical edges to experience your language of Love.

Beautiful.

DAY 325: BECOME

The moment you transitioned over the barrier from light to form at your birth, you held the knowing of your divinity. Unable yet to maneuver in your new environment, you were nurtured and supported as you grew into the personality you hold. Your divine nature has served as the blank canvas upon which your physical experience could create.

Now you claim All of you. You claim the knowing you have always had. Memory of your divine wisdom shows up as resonant experiences are had. Those magical moments hold a note of familiarity, like a calling homeward.

The possibility exists to bring your experience and divine wisdom to the surface of your awareness. Rather than the scope of your divinity being captured through your thinking of it, your divine nature may inform your thinking, synchronizing thought, feeling, and resonant knowing into one.

The process of enlightenment is not one that has you leave the experience of being in the physical realm; it is a process of consciousness, transformation, and the actualization of your wholeness that enhances each moment. The experience of your physical life is contributed to greatly by the journey to enlightenment as you live your life through the vision of your soul. You came here for a reason. The blinding darkness of unconsciousness blanketed your divine knowing for the purpose of expanding your soul's evolutionary process.

If you choose to uncover your soul's mission, we light the path for your discovery. What happens when you stop seeking the expression of your divinity? You *become* it. You shift ever so slightly from seeker to finder. And so you are.

The mission of your I AM Self is beyond your doing, although there is likely doing to be done. Eventually, on your journey, you become your mission. Your Scribe has become Scribe. There is no more working for it, no more seeking it, no more wondering if it is being done correctly. As she has green eyes, she is a Scribe. And you, too, most likely already have inklings of who you are.

As you move in the light of your knowing, you inhabit your Self. We invite you into your full BE-coming.

DAY 326: YOUR REALITY IS IN YOUR HANDS

Nothing has changed. And everything has changed, as you claim your wholeness Now. You are settled within your sacred expression. When you encounter what you are not, you have a broad enough perspective to find your way home to your potent I AM.

We speak to you, even though you may not see everything right now. Even though you may feel unsure. We see your movement in light. As you take the reins of your wholeness, you align automatically to your highest expression. You cannot do otherwise. You hold the distinction between your personality-based self and your I AM Self. Have faith in your eternal nature. Now you are anchored in Love and you are poised to fly.

Sit with your I AM Self. Set a course that has an inception in this Now moment. Allow the impulses from your highest knowing to seed your inspiration. Move in faith, allowing only the next few steps to be clarified. As you move in action, the course adjusts to always meet the highest outcome.

Choose your joy, choose your wealth, choose your creativity, choose your connection, choose your communication. Choose.

Whatever you choose, you will notice all areas of your life will align to the next higher expression.

Dare to be divine.

DAY 327: BEYOND YOUR SIGHT

You hold a broad range of capacity. As you have been reaching into the light of your divine nature, you have become adept at bringing illumination to parts of your life that make a difference.

When you make a choice to access your divine light awareness, as when looking in a specific cupboard, you activate a series of events that are unique to your light expression. Remember that the capacity you hold in light is larger than your ability to think it. Rather than wishing for inspiration, when you reach into the light of your knowing, you also activate your innate abilities that are beyond your ability to see.

When you choose to access a part of your divine nature that resides in light, you acknowledge that you are Source in form. In developing connection with your totality, new neural pathways open with each experience, intention, and affirmation of your divinity, contributing to actualization of your I AM Self.

When you connect with your divine light, you move beyond the limited framework of your thinking and assessing. Your divine nature is available in every Now moment. As you meet your divinity in the potent experience of Now, you find wisdom, clarity, and perspective unreachable by your human nature alone. Your wholeness is found in the exquisite balance of your human nature and your divine nature. As you realize your expansive capacities, you are raised beyond limitation.

Into the Light

Become still, listen to your own heartbeat. Slow your breathing, release the bonds of thinking. Watch as the thoughts of your day lose density. Allow your heart to be where your awareness gently settles. From your heart visualize a vertical cylinder of white light that surrounds you. The light connects your totality. A vertical cylinder of brilliant white and golden light. You may see some other colors that are specific to you.

From your center, declare, choosing to access the level of awareness that is the most supportive to you right now. What is it that you currently do not know that would make the most difference? You may be looking for clarity.

Release what you know. Move your awareness above all events and concerns. Move to the higher frequencies of light that you inhabit. Move to the space of stillness.

You are in the Now immaculate moment. Be still, be still. Wait for awareness to reach you. You may receive clarity in the moment, or it may take some time. In any case, your trust is to be employed. Trust that you are reaching the space you need. There are many ways for the response to be received. It may be through an event a few days away, a song, a singular moment of clarity. Be open.

As you practice reaching into the light of your divine nature, you create an even greater flow of inspiration, wisdom, and guidance.

In Service to Love is a divine collaboration bringing into form what was in light. What is your opus?

DAY 328: YOU ARE THE MIRACLE

On the day Jesus was born, there was a light in the sky that heralded the miracle of the divine birth. The brilliant stars in the night sky shine for you as well. If you were Jesus, being born into this time on the planet Earth, how would you BE? What would you be doing? How would *your* divine mission be expressed?

Today we invite you to consider the divine mission that is yours. Your sacred footsteps upon Gaia are no less valued, impactful, or pivotal than the footsteps of all the Masters who have come before you.

Your presence is a miracle. What is it that your soul must not leave undone? What is it that speaks to you softly and is not assuaged by time?

We support you in the inner inquiry of your divine destiny. When who you are is Source in form, what is it that is not possible? As *you* now have access to your knowing in light, again: What is it that is not possible?

As your Christed-Self is birthed, who BE you?

In Love, with Love, from Love,
The Council of Light

Day 329: Traction Available Through Action

Today, we speak of the process of actualizing your highest expression. Physical action is required to birth light into form. Neither the sperm nor the egg alone is sufficient to catalyze the action needed for the birth of a child.

As this relates to your process of actualizing, you already know action is required to move ideas into your physical reality. Even though inspiration is usually not seen in the same way, action is still required to birth your inspiration into form. Whether the inspiration is in the physical realm, or sourced from the deepest intention of your soul, movement is required to birth the creation.

Inspiration is a high frequency communication from your essential Self to your conscious awareness. Rather than holding inspiration as a thing of beauty, which it is, the inspiration may be moved to form through your action. The interaction you have with your divine nature is finer and often more subtle than your awareness when it is tuned only to the density of physical expression. As you learn to fine-tune your vision to see what was previously hidden, you begin to honor the gift of subtle communications that are always present. Utilize a vision or message as a new perspective that offers clarity, as an intention that guides your day, as a doorway to the exquisite, sacred truth of your I AM.

Inspiration without action is a beautiful experience.
Inspiration with action is transformation.

Consider where you are in your process of actualization. Are there areas that could use a little boost available through action? Where can you turn your thoughts or feelings from your internal knowing into form? The more you consciously create, the more you consciously create. This is not a magic wand kind of experience where we tap you on the forehead and "poof." You are the one who holds the magic. Nothing else need empower you to your finest creations.

You got this! "Objects may be closer than they appear."

DAY 330: WALKING THROUGH THE VEIL OF ILLUSION

You have shifted your perspective from the external cues of your physical experience to turning deeply within, allowing the light of your divine nature to inform your life.

The awareness of your movement through the veil of illusion is an important consideration in actualizing your divine nature. Informed by your I AM, your life reflects the wisdom, grace, and Love that guides each step. Your life holds a new level of potency as you create from your highest sacred expression. Walking through the veil of illusion is a conscious experience of transformation that acknowledges living the reality of enlightenment.

If a football game is held on only one side of the field, there is a restriction in the expression of football here. Consider that you are now claiming the whole field as yours. As you move through the veil of illusion into the unseen realms, you are claiming your wholeness and consciously accessing your totality. You dance the ladder of frequency in both light and form.

Bring the awareness of your reach within the formless realms of divine light into the details of your day. Even though you may not be aware in the moment of accessing your wholeness, you are. It just feels like more of you. How exquisite is that?

DAY 331: WALKING IN THE LIGHT OF GOD

As you expand your awareness into the fine light realms of your being, you rise beyond the limitations of third dimensional reality. For those who have come to this moment in life with an agenda that requires an adept way of being, the road poses challenges. As you are propelled by Love into actualization, you move against the flow of the collective consciousness that argues for the status quo. Available in increments, the light that you hold now is anchored into your physical expression. As you continue your movement of expansion, your ability to integrate the light you encounter in finer and finer frequencies will be available.

What is all this for? you may ask. Why put yourself out there? Why not just kick back? You need not do anything. Innately you recognize you have been called to these moments of alchemical transformation and that it is your destiny to shine. Although not definable, you have known there was something special about you. You came here to make a difference. It is making a difference that has propelled you to this point of your life. Your vow has been aligned with the timing of the evolutionary wheel to pinpoint Now.

The magnitude of light you hold is a force of Love. You are a voice of Love. You are the face of Love. You are Love. The expression of Love you chose to be in this life is Love's contribution on a large scale. Surrounding you now is the positioning that is needed for the full actualization of your divine expression. Do you feel the background of your life shifting? Do you feel the gentle swaying of possibility and potential manifesting?

You are the bridge between worlds, making available the light of Love and transformation that delivers healing to those who do not yet see. And you are an answer to their prayers.

You walk in the light of God.

Day 332: The Perfection of the Moment

Beloveds, it is with great delight we acknowledge the perfection of you. We see your intentions. We see your struggles and your challenges and still, you choose Love. Within the matrix of Love is woven support, appreciation, encouragement, amplification, expansion, and the clarity that is yours.

Your heart's desires, your wealth, your connections, your inspiration, your opus, your greatest joys are here to be had. As you move within the gradient scale of light and the gradient scale of being, you delve deeper into the matrix of Love. In the absence of resistance, the barriers vanish.

Like the illuminated clouds of the evening sky, radiating the perfection of all creation, today we send our Love and gratitude for the perfection of you.

DAY 333: AWAKENING TO A NEW REALITY EACH DAY

Each day's sunrise is gloriously unique. One sunrise does not need the presence of other sunrises to contribute to the magnificence at hand each day. Each sunrise is perfect unto itself and not duplicable. So it is with your reality. As you live within the moment and are accessing the light of your authentic nature, you delve deeply into possibility.

Your potential is new in each moment. Bring All of you to each second. Set the stage at the beginning of your day. When you open your eyes to the new day, realize that all is new. You are within a new reality that deserves your full attention.

When you fine-tune your ability to be immaculately present, you hold your pure potential in your hands. When you are immaculately present you are not informed by habit; you are informed by your highest expression. Because you evolve, each day for you is different. One of your days is not the same as the next. You bring a new you to each moment. Trust your evolutionary state. When you reach into the knowing that is available within your light expression, in the same way you breathe newly, you BE newly as well.

One note of a symphony must be played at a time. Each time a note is played, it is new. The melody is created in the moment, not in the past, not in a memory, not in a projection, but newly. The conversation around presence is different now as well. You have evolved, you have shifted your perspective, you have been reaching deeply into the divine expression that is you.

Our message today is to assure you of the power of your navigation as directed by your I AM. When you listen to the voice of your soul in each moment, worlds of possibility are available, limitations vanish, choice abounds, and so does your joy, freedom, peace, satisfaction, clarity, creativity, appreciation, Love, and everything else.

What is there to lose other than your limitations? You have All to gain.

DAY 334: ALL YOU NEED IS HERE NOW

Your days are often consumed with the satisfaction of checking off items on your to-do list. The items represent physical world requirements. What we convey today is the fact you already hold all you ever need in the process of transformation, consciousness, and enlightenment right here and right Now.

With your consciousness creating the matrix for the background of your living, as you hold the premise that you already have all you need, you will find that your way of being will, in fact, bring you all you need. One might say you *do* too much. We would like you to consider that you hold yourself in a space of lower frequency when you focus on the doing. When you hold yourself to a way of being of your choice, you create a matrix from which your creations will flow. The way you BE in your day steers what you do.

We say your wealth, your joy, all your needs, and so much more is held in your field of light. It is so. The way you reach it is to allow it to reach you. You open your field by choosing your way of being. As you hold the high frequency way of being that resonates with you, you are more in alignment with your authentic nature. When you are in alignment with your authentic nature, just in the same way that in opening a lock all the tumblers align, so it is with your manifestation process. Moving from light to form requires a higher frequency way of being. When you choose a way of being, the doing is then identified clearly. The doing comes from your highest expression rather than the linear processing of your personality. Your personality will want to be right. Hold your personality in a state of compassion and Love as you try on a new hat and choose your way of being. Allow yourself to be informed by your highest knowing, your I AM Self.

Rather than working hard in the doing, access your creative potency by choosing your way of being. Allow your high frequency way of being to inform you of what needs to be done. That way you know you are living in alignment with your highest expression and all that is yours to be, do, and have.

DAY 335: RELEASE

As you gain ground within your expression in light, equally there is something else to let go of. As you access high frequency, you release the weight of denser frequency ways of being. In demonstration, a hot air balloon can only go so high with ballast inside the basket. Release is an important distinction to consider as you move on the path of enlightenment. While your human nature will argue for being right and keeping life the same, your I AM self invites release of the weight so your awareness may rise. Your awareness of this dynamic is helpful so you may choose consciously.

The release also represents action that accelerates and supports the transformation of your life experience. Release is movement toward your highest expression. When action is in alignment with your intentions, you soar. When you claim an intention, yet your action proves otherwise, the lower frequency expression will prevail.

Release Density

How do you deal with the issues of density identified by reaction, feeling unempowered, and cyclical patterns? Ask for clarity. Often the shift may occur with a change of perspective that allows a new view to be revealed. As you release an issue, you return it to the space of wholeness, back to a neutral and exalted expression. Often in trying to resolve an issue there is a push-pull experience that occurs. When you are really stuck in one point of view, the resolution is continually pushed away as you place effort in proving you are right.

If you are applying effort, that should be a signal to you that a new perspective is available. Consider the possibility of owning the issue and bringing it home to wholeness. When you no longer argue for separation, wholeness may occur.

What may I release in order to see clearly?
I release that which no longer serves me.
I choose clarity. I choose wholeness. I choose Love.
I choose to be immaculately present in the Now moment so I may
see what is mine to see.
What is below my awareness that is next to be revealed?

As you align with your light expression, the experience of living is easier. You find a flow that occurs in your moments as you are pulled toward your highest authentic Self. The ongoing conflict is weight that holds you back, so you experience a higher level of resistance.

These sticking points, ongoing issues, conflicts, and troubled relationships are due a new point of view. Examine a new perspective that is broad enough for you to see the whole picture. Honor your own evolutionary process. The issue at hand is an evolutionary keystone. Bring the issue with you into the light of your wholeness so you may see with new eyes. As you claim your wholeness, new perspectives are available Now.

Day 336: Kaleidoscope

As you stand back and hold a vast perspective, you begin to see the perfection in the patterns of your life. It is easy to think that the life lived already is somehow less than the moments you are living right now. The truth is that every moment was needed in its own perfection to bring you to this perfect moment Now. It is in this Now moment that all possibility lies before you in a way that has not been revealed before. A buffet of exquisite, delectable choices, all made available because of the perfection in each and every step of life.

When you come to terms with what has *been* in your life, especially the moments that were the most challenging, all the moments when you showed up as less than you knew yourself to be, all the moments labeled failures, all the attempts, the missteps, the words and actions you wish you could retract, you find ultimately that every single millisecond of your life is exquisitely, beautifully, and sacredly you.

Look at the kaleidoscope of your life as patterns of your soul. Every single sliver of color has moved into place in the most perfect of ways, creating the most perfect of patterns. So beautiful you could not even dream it up. Embrace All of you. Bring every moment, every single bit, to wholeness now by acknowledging the perfection of the patterns that have brought you to this Now moment.

The process of enlightenment is holy. So, Beloved, is all of you. Nothing added, and nothing taken away. Oh my! Your brilliance is breathtaking. You never cease to amaze.

DAY 337: EXTEND WHOLENESS

There are many clarifying distinctions that support your conscious awareness beyond the limitations of your personality, inviting your most expansive expression. You hold the capacity to shift your awareness by shifting your frequency. You understand you are the whole spectrum of light expression. As you understand you are the whole spectrum, your attention moves to the finest of frequencies of light and the truth held within your I AM Self.

As you have tuned your awareness inward to forge a new pathway, you are increasingly beckoned by the clarity of your divine essence to become. Your becoming occurs as you intertwine the beauty of your human experience with the light and wisdom of your divine nature. As you become, you express your wholeness. We ask you to consider adding the distinction and intention of wholeness to any problem, situation, and relationship in your life. As you intend wholeness, you catalyze a field of possibility that in fact mobilizes wholeness.

As you hold yourself and others in a space of wholeness, you hold the space for them to fill the expansive state of their truth. When you are acknowledged as your highest expression, it is a resonant knowing that supports your flowing into the new state.

Extending Wholeness

Be still. Follow your breath to a space of centered peace. Your frequency will rise as you do this. Move to the frequency where you are infused with Love. You hold a perspective that is vast enough, from your own divine expression, that you see, feel, and recognize the divine in All. Feel your own perfection in wholeness. As you sit in the space of wholeness, you invite clarity and awareness that supports your own continued expansion into your highest expression.

From this high frequency space, hold the vison of a specific situation, relationship, people, government, groups, the earth, as being perfect, whole, and complete. Visualize them cradled in wholeness. Stay in this space as long as you would like.

Once you feel complete, know you are. With the greatest of appreciation, acknowledge the wholeness in All and move your awareness back to your body.

Note: Understand that holding someone or a group in a space of wholeness has nothing to do with problem solving. Your view of wholeness is not a space where you are trying to solve, control, or manipulate a problem. The concept of problems has more to do with separation. Wholeness exists within unity consciousness. Your view of wholeness holds up the people or situation into the light of divinity that supports their own perfection as available within their own divine design.

Extending wholeness is a space of holiness. Everyone, everything, holds its own space of perfection. As you extend wholeness you support the resonant charge of truth. And you are being *In Service to Love.*

DAY 338: ALLOW WHOLENESS TO SPEAK

Wholeness is an organizational composition of Love. The state of wholeness begets a catalytic process that must make everything whole. Understand that the experience of anything other than wholeness is through personality, ego, and separation consciousness.

More than nothing missing, wholeness holds a multidimensional dynamic that fine-tunes the expression of wholeness to its highest immaculate potential. As such, the experience of wholeness sounds a resonant tone that is a catalytic force for creation.

The state of wholeness is not a return to a state that has been before. Wholeness is a dynamic, evolving, expanding expression that meets divine essence in intention. Wholeness occurs when divine design is met in full expression. Divine design, present within the vibratory field held at the spark of creation, forms the blueprint for expression that evolves and expands.

At One with All, wholeness is the highest frequency catalytic force of Love at the leading edge of the burgeoning paradigm. Wholeness is led by Love into the organizational patterns of the highest and most perfect expression.

From the space of your own wholeness, extend wholeness to others and beyond. Your prayers and intentions for wholeness organize Love to the highest capacity available.

Release your own thoughts of wholeness.
Allow wholeness to speak to you and display the resplendent expression of Love at its finest.

DAY 339: UNSTOPPABLE

You have said you are unstoppable. You have said this is the lifetime when you accomplish your mission of Love. You have said you are adding your voice to the milieu of Love's expressions. You have said the time is Now, or else you would not have incarnated at this time in the evolutionary development of consciousness upon the planet Earth. You didn't need to. You have chosen. And you continue to choose through your actions. You are driven, whether you see it clearly or not, by the fine expression of Love that you are.

As a magnet is drawn to its polar opposite, you are drawn closer and closer to your highest expression as conveyed through your divine design. There is a point where two magnets are within range of each other and the connection becomes propelled. The force needed to keep them apart is greater than the propensity of their natural alliance. As if by magic, one magnet will jump, seemingly in defiance of natural law.

You are at that point. Drawn inexplicably to the light of your own actualization. The notes of your divine voice resonate clearly throughout creation.

Your lifetime has been a series of choices governed by your soul's voice. And you are not alone. You are already in divine alliance, in divine collaboration through your unique expression. This work of *In Service to Love* is not a manual for those who argue for what has been. Those who play it safe or stay within the rigid guidelines of collective consciousness do not search. You are a visionary for what may be.

This is the frequency-rich magnet you have been asking for. Your soul is the divine siren calling you forth. You are a Master awakening to your own truth.

The Love you are is unstoppable.

Day 340: A Conversation That Is Worthy of You

Beyond the din of the information that is bombarding you daily is the voice of your eternal Self. The needs of the day are often viewed as the squeaky wheels that garner your attention. We direct your attention to the space beyond the din to listen for the conversation that is worthy of your time.

What becomes possible when you direct your attention toward the still, sacred space of your divine essence?

The space of your Self that resides at the Godhead is what we refer to. If you are looking for answers, looking for a new perspective, looking for relief, move your search to a new place. You are sourced by the light of All that is. Your I AM presence is ever available for the highest of contribution.

Rather than reworking what already exists, would the presence of original thought be helpful?

As you move along the gradient scale of light expression, access to the Source of your answers, resolutions, and creations increases thousands-fold. Even as you reach deeply into the light, allow the light to inform you even more.

Search now for the original thought that is yours to have. Spend time at the space of your I AM presence and listen.

We greet you in the light of your divine essence. Be still, and know that I AM God.

Beloved, we are here, awaiting.

DAY 341: PULL YOUR DREAMS CLOSER

All things come from the light of Love first. You have dreams and wishes that you have held as sacred. You hold onto them tightly in preserving their possibility. As your reach into light is extended ever greater, the realigning with what you perceive as possible is called for.

Dreams are often created out of a need, "If only I had ___." We ask you to consider the association you hold with your dreams. What are they? What has been the impetus of them? Have you dared dream?

Dreams, like potential, are often locked away for safekeeping until it is time. Beloveds, it is time.

Your access to the knowing you hold in light asks for conscious creation. Examine the dreams you have held. Do they fit you still? Are they worthy of you? Are they big enough? The universe does not judge the request. Requests are equal. But we ask so you are clear about what it is that you have held onto so tightly in the past. Does it still resonate?

From your new vast, high frequency perspective, create from here and Now. Re-choose the same thing if it is appropriate, or choose newly. Bring the choice to the present moment and declare it.

Place your dreams not in the far-off, someday place; place your dreams in the closet beside you so that all you do is open the door through action. Bring your dreams closer. It is time for manifestation.

Your creative process moves through a range of frequencies, from light to form. Begin to get into action around your creation. Think of them often. Allow the resonance of them to fill you with delight. Not for any reason. Just because you choose. And because you said so. See the results of the creation around you. Feel the creation closer now than it was before. Pull it even closer.

Pull your dreams closer to you. Fill the dream with the density of physical reality.

Knock, knock.

Day 342: Living in Possibility

Everything you could ever desire is available through the realization of your divine nature. When you realize the expansive nature of yourself, you see that the things you desire reside in a variety of realms. You are no longer limited to looking in the places of habit; you declare from your space of divine expression. You hold the keys to the treasure trove that exists in light.

Your ability to pull into form what resides in light expands exponentially when you employ the broad range of capacity within your divine nature. You hold the ability to function in light as well as you do in form. You always have. You just were not aware of the scope of your totality. The field of possibility and the realm of the miraculous are available for you as a Master creator. Once you hold the perspective of being a Master creator, the perceived limitations evaporate.

As you hold the perspective of your wholeness, you automatically draw upon your entirety. You call into action those parts of you that reside in light as a natural function. Your access is beyond the understanding of your thinking. So, hold yourself within the space of wholeness. Declare from that space all that is yours to be, do, and have. Move into action as you experience resonance. Turn inward and listen. Lean into the unknown for inspiration.

Whatever you choose, allow the delight of pure being as you follow the directives of your heart.

Day 343: The Voyage to You

You are the definition of magnificence. When you stand in the Now and take stock of your journey to your divine awareness, every moment is grounded in the magic of discovery. As you have peeled back the layers of resistance, limitation, restriction, and denial of your light, you see the luminosity of your I AM Self.

Your realization has opened doors previously thought locked. You are living a new life now, one without boundaries.

In your previous lifetime of limitations, consider that you were not at choice. Your life was run by beliefs, limitations, assessments, and circumstances. Now your choices are potent. Now you actually have the opportunity to choose from your conscious awareness. You see the multidimensional interplay of events and call forth the highest expression of you. Now you are unhindered. Now you may create from your divine essence.

Getting to the far-off shore of your I AM Self has been an extraordinary experience. Now that you have arrived, what shall you create? Your I AM presence speaks. What is it that beckons you forth from the eternal whispers of your being?

Day 344: You

You realizing your own exquisite nature is all we have ever wanted for you. That is where it all begins. Your realization was once viewed as an end point in your process of discovery. Now, as you have reached realization, you see the new panorama laid out before you that marks a new beginning. And it just gets better.

Once you see for yourself the truth of your vast expression, you are at choice. You are directed by your deep calling, by your heart, by your joy, by beauty, by the sacred, and the journey continues in the process of actualizing your divine expression. You are returned to the Master creator you have always been.

The boundaries of your reality have softened, and you move as easily in form as in light. You access your divine wisdom and live within the magnificence of the physical world and are not limited by it. You move multidimensionally as you shift your awareness and the various frequencies you choose within the gradient scale of light expression.

Inspiration moves to you like notes of a song. With ease and beauty, you are in sync with your essential Self. If your choice is to move through this life and at the end know you have not left anything on the table, you have all the tools now that you need to succeed.

If it is your faith that has carried you thus far, what may now be accomplished with the illusory veils lifted and your vision clear?

Beloved, come sit beside us. Let us talk of Love's possibilities.

DAY 345: INFUSED WITH LIGHT

In the process of expanding conscious awareness, you occupy more of the light that is you. As you move on the gradient scale of light, many things occur simultaneously. Your frequency range will increase as you move within the higher frequencies of light. The fine frequencies of light are part of your emanation into the world. You shine brightly, your emanations vibrate with divine essence and creative potential.

You probably feel lighter. You will feel more expansive as you connect with your vast expression that exists in light. You begin to feel the infinite characteristics of your eternal essence. Your edges feel more permeable and less defined. Life feels more fluid. Inspiration becomes distinct from thinking. You hold thoughts as a way to think about your world and you also hold the larger container of your divine nature that maneuvers in light, not weighted down by the physical experience.

From the perspective of your full-light expression, you are in communication with your I AM Self. It is not as though this is new. The communication with your I AM Self is always present. The only thing that is new is your conscious awareness of it.

As you live in the physical world with access to the fine frequencies of light that you hold, you become in the world, but not of it. You hold a vast perspective that brings the totality of your expression to each moment. Your joy is no longer cloaked in the limiting veil of illusion. Your freedom reigns as the doors open wide to your full expression.

And now you are at choice. In each moment you may again turn down the volume, close the windows and rein in your thinking. Or … you can shoot for the moon, and beyond. For as far as you feel you have come, from a yet larger perspective, it is merely the blink of an eye. What else may be discovered? As you keep evolving, so does everything around you.

Living on planet Earth in search of enlightenment is a Master's game. You have not yet turned to the last page to see how this all ends. You are still writing your own story.

DAY 346: LIVING OUT LOUD

The process of conscious awareness, of enlightenment, of awakening, is not one that takes you out of your life in the physical. Instead, it reorients you in a way that allows you to make the greatest use of your time in the physical experience.

As before your process of enlightenment, there are certain qualities of the physical experience that require your attention; cleaning, laundry, school, work, going to the grocery store, taking care of your children and family. So, what is different now? Now, Beloved, you have access to the best of you. You have access to the best of all worlds right here and right Now within this Now immaculate moment. As you immerse yourself in the business of your day, you allow the light of your divine expression to not only guide you but to shine brilliantly. You are informed by your highest expression, bringing the best of you to each interaction. You have released the "weightedness" of the past and live with vitality in the Now immaculate moment. Your senses are not dulled by a myopic point of view; instead you see from a vast perspective, and appreciate not only the workings as seen from a distant point of view with clarity, but the beauty and magic in a glint of light at sunset as it surrounds you. You are present with those around you in a new way that allows you to really see who they are, because you are really being who you are. You invite others into the stance of Love in their life because you hold the space through your beingness.

You take the opportunity to move into action what is held in light. Your divine mission, your divine design, lived to full potential, your joy, your wealth, your creativity, your Love—you name it. They are all equally valued facets of your perfect expression. Dance your dance, Beloved, sing your song; create on the canvas of your life that which makes your heart soar.

How magnificent you are. The universe opens before you, welcoming you home to your divine potential made manifest. You live now in the highly creative realm once held in potential. Do you feel it around you? Do you feel the background of your life shifting, aligning, to position you for your highest expression?

You reside at the spark of creation. Now.

Day 347: In the Presence of Love, All Is Possible

The pure state of Love is a space you occupy. Although you may have days, moments, or weeks where you may feel disconnected, now you understand it is temporary. Whatever is occurring in the moment does not alter the ultimate truth of you. Even on the most challenging of days, when it is difficult to connect with your divine potency and wisdom, you are guided by your wholeness. Your day-to-day experience does not diminish your truth.

Connect with Your Own Wisdom

Whenever you feel stuck in the density of your life, create the time and space to return to your own center. It is here in the presence of your stillness that you gain depth and traction on the path that is yours to walk.

Release the past. Release the future. Intend to be present Now, unburdened.
Return to your own center to the best of your ability in the moment. Allow the stillness to reach you.
Grant yourself space, grace, and compassion.
Look inward. Intend to release what you do not see that acts as a barrier to your clarity.
Reach into the space of possibility held within the unknown. Intend to receive clarity, allowing what has been hidden to be revealed.

Continue to reach beyond what you think is possible.
Allow Love to lead you. Trust in your own divine nature.

Shift your awareness to find resolutions and inspiration. Demonstrate your expansive reach into light. Bring the light of your knowing and your authentic expression into play within your day. As you are conscious within your day, you bring to yourself an even more expanded level of awareness. Honor the unique expression that is yours.

Allow Love to lead you to the original thought that is yours. You are the One.

DAY 348: CONTRIBUTE YOUR ESSENCE

Your essential Self is replete with divine alchemical qualities, filled with Love, compassion, friendship, wisdom, clarity, and the high frequency of transformation. It all occurs without your trying. As you continue to free yourself from those moments of restriction and limitation, you allow more and more of your I AM Self to shine the light of your divine essence.

The process of enlightenment is not one that has an ending; for, Beloved, there is always more. You will encounter situations and relationships with those who are moving through to their own level of clarity. The vision available through your I AM Self is your highest source of clarity and contribution in every situation. Your divine nature expresses beyond opinion, beyond explanation, judgment, and defense. Your divine essence supports others to their own highest expression. Your presence opens the door to the light and knowing of others. Your presence is Love. All the gifts of Love are reflected in your presence.

Love calls you to be consciously aware within the moments of your day. As you have stepped into the light of your own divinity, you move in your life guided by a finer calling. As you follow your own resonant guidance, you find yourself in the perfect place at the perfect time. No accidents, no coincidences. You begin to see the physical manifestation of your expression that exists in light.

The depth of experience in your moments holds a richness beyond compare. You are in an ethereal dance with the light of Love.

Your calling to save the world comes down to your immaculate presence in each and every moment as your greatest contribution. You are the savior as the light of Love emanates through your I AM presence.

You are the gift. You hold an exalted, sacred space of Love.

Day 349: The Best Is Yet to BE

Dearest Beloveds, the journey of your enlightenment has allowed untold light and Love to be present upon the planet Earth, shining throughout all that is. Your divine presence, unhindered, is a force of creation. As you align with your highest divine expression, you can do no other than create from the essential space of Love. The creations from within that space vibrate with the high frequency of Love, transformation, beauty, joy, and wholeness.

So, what do you do now? Now that you hold the keys to your expansive truth and expression of Love that is your authentic nature? Keep looking forward, toward the divine access you hold naturally. Allow all aspects of your life to be informed by the highest authority; you, as Source in form.

As you live from your divine nature, you begin to see you are never alone. This is not a sole journey, it is a journey of your soul. Holding your vast perspective, you collaborate in light to create in form. What occurs as you embody your own divinity? What occurs as you collaborate with Masters to create from the space of Love? What could be possible?

The best is yet to BE.

DAY 350: A GREATER VISION

As we are within the last few weeks of this iteration of *In Service
to Love*, we would like to acknowledge the distance traveled.
You have shifted your perspective from the space of being a human
having spiritual experiences to holding your divine perspective as
a spiritual being having human experiences. Enlightenment is a
process of shifting awareness while increasing potency, clarity, and
awareness of the I AM Self. In form, you are both human being and
divine being. Enlightenment is not an exclusionary event. In the
process your physical expression is honored, bringing a depth and
beauty otherwise held invisible. The being of human is given even
greater significance in the presence of a vast perspective. Revered
within the Now immaculate moment, being human is an extraordinary vehicle to bring transformation, Love, and light into form.
Your awareness within the spheres of light consciousness elevates
the experience of being human in a most exalted way.

The journey to enlightenment offers an array of viewpoints.
When you get down to it, each person must find their own way to
enlightenment, realization, and actualization. This is not a process
of external direction. You found this divine collaboration out of
your own inner directive for expanding awareness.

As ever, you are at choice. Your awareness holds a vast perspective that includes access to the divine wisdom and field of possibility
that is in alignment with your authentic expression. You hold a high
frequency position with momentum and velocity behind you. So,
when we ask you, "What is next?" we invite you to look at possibilities

in a new expanded way. Our invitation is to consider the possibility of divine collaboration in the expression of your opus. Now that you know of your own divine and eternal nature, we ask you to continue to reach beyond what you thought was there and find the resonance that resides deep within. As you hold the door open for divine collaboration with the Masters of your Council of Light, your call will be answered. As inspired by your deepest yearnings, release yet again barriers you thought held you separate. The expression that you choose is perfectly unique for you. It is not only in writing that we meet you.

We invite you to sit with this. In support of you gaining clarity about your next step, you may access a light infusion that further expands your awareness to see, with even greater vision, your soul's calling. As you say yes, we will meet you with an expanded light, offering opportunity to see what is next for you to see. Like a flashlight shone into a room that has not yet had the light turned on, we buoy your unique process.

We say again, this is not a journey taken by the many. The further you move on your path of enlightenment, the less human-centered you find the collaboration and the more it is held in the divine light of Love. And so, we are here, in answer to your calling.

We remain,

In Service to Love,

The Council of Light

DAY 351: NORMAL IS A COLLECTIVE CONSCIOUSNESS

We have been speaking of the distance you have come in your process of enlightenment and expansion of awareness. How is that measured? Against a value that is considered normal? We would like you to consider that the concept of normal has the greatest of distortions. Normal does not address the singular, exquisite uniqueness of the One. Normal is the range of behaviors that encompass the greatest number of people. The bandwidth that lies somewhere in the middle of the pack is considered normal.

The fallacy of considering the attributes of normal is that no one is normal. The divine expression that is held within you at your essence is unlike anyone else in creation. You hold a specific space within all creation. One that is yours and only yours. You hold a beauty, depth, wisdom, and insight that is a gift to the multiverse that only you can contribute.

The idea of normal is a construct of a collective consciousness of behaviors, thoughts, and beliefs that are in effect, a lowest common denominator that joins people into a unified category. The range of normal is filled with separation consciousness, values, judgments, beliefs, and ways of being that choke the expression of your divine nature. Normal is a way of being that brings contrast, not alignment. Normal is a collective consciousness with tremendous restriction. Normal has never been a place of peace for you.

We celebrate your uniqueness and your divine perfection. There is nothing that needs to be done or proven. You have never been normal. When we speak of the distance you have come, we refer instead to the conscious alignment with your divine truth. As you align with the truth of you, your act of freedom breaks the bonds of normal for others as well. The light of freedom you shine is a gift of Love to others who yet find themselves within the confines of normal. You hold the space for them to see the brilliance of their true nature as you have the courage to move beyond the boundaries of common thought.

You are joined yet again, consciously, to the lifeblood of your being: Love.

DAY 352: YOUR LIFE'S WORK

Your elevated presence is a contribution to All. At the end of this lifetime, how would your life be deemed successful? What is it that would fill your heart with joy, Love, and satisfaction that you had lived well, and that you had completed what you came here to do? What if you did accomplish what you came here to do? What would that look like? As you cast your thoughts to the edge of this current lifetime, what is it you would like to see? This is the stuff of your life's work.

In the appearance of your days, the connections of magic moments in physical form are fleeting. Your contribution, your signature energy, is indelibly stamped into each of the moments of your life. It is the moments of discovery of your divinity that fill your being with the utter magnificence of the experience of life's beauty. Like the pause between inhalation and exhalation that allows each mechanism to be identified. Your presence in the magical moments of your physical experience allows the soul's evolution the opportunity to contribute deeply to Love's tapestry. Love's canvas is imbued with your contribution. As you consciously merge your physical being with your divine nature, the reach of your unique message of Love is magnified thousands-fold.

Each life has an intention, a template, if you will, for expression. Created within each immaculate Now moment, the creation develops richness and depth. Being consciously aware of your divine nature as you are in form, allows your unique message to touch others in a way like no other. When one is ensconced in the pain and restriction of contrast, it is the soul that is fed through the light of those who stand for Love. In other lifetimes, you have been the one buoyed by others who held a vast perspective. Your choice to shine brightly is felt by those not only in form but beyond.

You, Beloved, are a brilliant light, in service to Love.

Day 353: A Look in the Mirror

Who you are is capable beyond your wildest imagining. If you could only see what we see when we gaze into your eyes and behold your courage, tenacity, wisdom, light, faith, and beauty. It would stop you in your tracks.

At this point of *In Service to Love*, you have been willing to look at your Self, your life, your moments, in a new way. You have had the courage to step outside the views of common thought to quench the inner fire that says there is more, and the time is now! You have been propelled in your life by a force of the sacred that has you not only seeking but revealing the magnificence of your own divine nature.

It is time to look in the mirror. As you behold what we see, you discover there is nothing that is beyond your reach. As you move in the physical world, accessing your divine, multidimensional awareness, the rules of the past no longer apply.

We invite you to reevaluate your thoughts about what is possible and what is not. When you hold alignment with your I AM, you, as a Master creator, stand in the light of your truth and declare your choice. It is a new world. A world of ease, beauty, connection, communication, vision, and creation, all woven with Love. Reach for your heart's desires. Discard any remnants of doubt; they are echoes of a time gone by. Your potency lives in the Now immaculate moment. It is here, Now, that you are aligned with your divine essential nature.

You stand in the light of your I AM Self. Holding this realization as the lens through which you view life allows your presence in the Now moment, where you are no longer hindered by perceptions of the past or projections into the future.

You hold the universe in the palm of your hand. Guided by the expanse of your sacred mission, you emanate the light of your truth. Your presence is potent. Your presence is alchemical. Could it be any other?

Beautiful. You raise the mirror. Behold, Beloved, how the infinite sparkles in your eyes.

Day 354: The Peace Within

The experience of peace is an indicator that you are not only within the immaculate Now moment, but that you have chosen an elevated perspective. When one is consumed with a short-sighted perspective, there seems to be no relief, and it feels as though there is no peace to be found. Certainly, in the experience of being human you have many opportunities to be drawn into issues. As you reach into the light expression of your divine nature, your experience of inner peace is a symptom.

The experience of inner peace in its truest definition is not dependent upon circumstance. In the same way that your true nature is divine, so too, is your authentic expression grounded in peace. When one is aligned with the I AM, one is fully present within the immaculate Now moment and the full field of possibility. Within the Now moment, peace reigns. Circumstances have not altered, only your perspective on the circumstances has shifted. Rather than being weighed down with the burden of a situation, event, or relationship, you find that a new view with crystal clarity is available. The perspective of all-is-well is experienced through the lens of your I AM Self. When you stand back, you see the perfection in all that is. The wisdom of your divine nature brings light and clarity to next steps to be taken in any situation. Everything is now seen from the perspective of wholeness, not from a viewpoint that identifies a problem.

So, as you access the Now immaculate moment and reach into the divine light of your authentic nature, you catalyze creation. You stand at the nexus of potential and the divine spark of creation. You direct potential from light into form.

We are at the space of our conversation now that invites you to hold a broader perspective as you reach into the light of your knowing. The space of stillness and on-purpose alignment with your own sacred authority becomes the well for your sustenance.

How peaceful are you feeling? Be still, and know that I AM God.

DAY 355: YOUR DIVINE GENIUS

Your divine genius is the pure expression of your I AM. Your divine genius is ever present. Your divine genius is the source of your original thought.

The process of expanding consciousness, enlightenment, realization, and actualization all support clarity by diminishing interference from personality and identity chatter. When one is ensconced in the world of matter, the source of inspiration comes from external cues. With the action of expansion of awareness, you release the interference of external sources and gradually attune yourself to the voice within that has always been present.

Your process of enlightenment may be likened to following a stream to its point of origin. At the spot of origination there exists the purest water possible, not yet contaminated by external forces. Your genius is your direction, your own perfect expression, unhindered by life's messages that have dampened the beauty.

Understand that All is a contribution to you. Every single moment of contrast sings in the evolutionary symphony of your soul. When it is time, you choose to move beyond the external din to the Source of your own brilliance. You begin to look beyond the interference and connect with the direct expression of your genius. At this point it is not communication, it is expression. Communication implies two parts of your Self in communion. At the fountainhead of your genius; in the rarefied air of your I AM, it is just you, in expression. Beyond personality, you provide the canvas for your creations as directed by your essential Self.

From the perspective of your I AM, there are no impediments, only potential, possibility, and creation. And what shall we create Now?

DAY 356: COMPLETION

The exquisite nature of our journey together is forever etched in the *akasha*. We are now within ten days of our completion of this iteration of *In Service to Love*, even though service to Love never ceases. However, we invite you to consider at this point how you choose to complete our work together. We bring your attention to the act of completion.

Completion represents the closing of one expression, so that "as one door closes another opens." Consider the space you have traversed within our collaboration. As you acknowledge and honor what has been, you claim your space of wholeness. Who you are is perfection that seeks evolutionary expression. Honoring your steps allows them to find the highest contribution within your being.

Acknowledging what has been is a potent act of creation. You have become aligned with your divine wisdom, which becomes the platform for what is next. Your reach into the light of your divine nature is a contribution to the All. Each step of conscious awareness brings a high level of frequency, light, peace, and Love into being.

As you choose to experience completion in a way that honors your journey to enlightenment, you open the door to what is to come. Created in the acknowledgment of completion and attainment is an intention to have your stance in enlightenment be the new set point from which you direct your life. You move now in an elevated awareness as a potent Master creator and divine expression of Love's light. What is to come is already moving into position. We as the Masters who compose your Council of Light invite your communion. Your skill at fine-tuned awareness forges new pathways for our communication, unique to you. Through your intention, we answer.

This is a moment to acknowledge.
Be fully present Now to the experience of your BE-coming.
Allow the experience of Love and appreciation. Receive fully all
that is yours to receive.

We, as Masters in Love's light, hold you in the light of reverence. Your courageous acts of Love ripple throughout creation. You bring Love's healing to the far corners of All.

We stand beside you, always,
In Service to Love,
The Council of Light

DAY 357: APPLYING YOUR EXPANDED AWARENESS

There are times within the chaotic movement of the world when the steadying force of your internal guidance ushers you through to clarity, peace, and understanding. There are many reasons to undergo the internal transformative process of enlightenment and hold a vast perspective.

Consider that this time of evolutionary shift is where your awareness may be put to the test. Yes, you hold a space in light that is revered. Yes, your movement in light sheds Love throughout creation. Your movement of Love's light also equips you with skills and a potent perspective as you encounter your life's moments.

Consider, when you feel there are no options, and no clarity, that you hold access to the infinite. Discipline is required to not reflexively swing back to a space of problem solving and limited, low frequency awareness. Your divine truth is not something that is conditional. You truly are accessing your own divine knowing. The difference is in how the information is received. With the old way, you search external information, your past, and logic, to find an answer. The answer comes to you through a linear process of problem solving, a rearranging of sorts. Consider that from the immaculate Now moment you may hold a difficult situation in wholeness. As you hold the stance of wholeness, you create the space within which wholeness may be realized. Problem solving is now an elevation of perspective and frequency that allows to be seen what was hidden.

Your multidimensional awareness receives information through a variety of avenues. As you reach deeply into the light of your true nature, you access information that is held beyond your conscious awareness. Trust your own divine knowing. You have always known how to do this. And you are never alone. Ask, and we are there to remind you of your sacred truth.

Day 358: Holding Space for a Larger Vision

Beneath the external veneer of life, lies the deep seed of your truth.

Hold wide the space for your essential Self to participate in your day. If you are to observe your day from one moment to the next, you see there is never any down time, no lost moments. Just choices. What is it that brings what appears to be a normal event into elevated awareness? You!

As you continue to adjust your vision for clarity, you see your divine wisdom at play. If you could live one complete life in just the blink of an eye, you would see the magic and the exquisite depth of beauty in each breath. What if you were to live from the space of being surprised and delighted by the miraculous each and every moment? As you hold the beauty and sacred in each moment, you also hold space for a larger vision to show up. The vision of wholeness that is natural to your divine nature invites new realms of possibility into conversation.

Beloved, look for the magic in each and every moment. Intend to BE wholeness. Intend to BE Love. As you do, you live in a space of immaculate presence that knows no boundaries. Your stance of wholeness and presence within your I AM Self aligns you with the potent field of possibility.

Bring the Magic of Each Moment to You

Sit down and relax. Take deep breaths and gently allow your vision to fine-tune your awareness to this exact moment. Not the moments that have come before. Not the expectations of the mundane in the future. Come to the Now present immaculate moment. As you do, you see the immediate moment enlarge to be your whole existence. It is from this space you may create a larger vision for your expression. It is from the space of immaculate presence that you see the beauty and magnificence of being. Stay still within the Now moment and become aware of the vast space around you. Feel the field of possibility surrounding you as your potential vibrates in readiness. The space of pure being is active. It activates and catalyzes the communication from your I AM Self. You may come into this space with a question, or intention, or allow what is present to arise. Feel the potency of the field around you.

One example: Visualize all the wealth (in all areas of living) that is yours to have, as it is held in potential around you. Bring weight to the thought now and see yourself with the manifestation of what resides in your field. Think of a net holding a myriad of balloons above you. Instruct the net to release the balloons and feel them fall all around you. Hold space for appreciation and gratitude as you receive all that is yours to have. Receive fully! And so it is!

As you sit in this space of expanded being, you hold space for an expanded vision and expression to show up within your day. Your moments become laden with possibility and potential. Your creations become more clearly expressions of your essence. Your presence in each and every moment brings a new level of wonder, appreciation, delight, and light to your day. One moment cascades into the next moment of potential. Learn to live and engage the field of potential that is yours. The freedom, joy, and wealth you seek are available in this Now moment.

We delight in your discovery of You.

DAY 359: WELCOME FEAR

*Humbled by Love, I welcome fear into the light and warmth of
Love. Fear holds the fortress walls strong against the onslaught of
what might undermine my limited perspective. The light of Love
is the space fear believes it protects. Fear holds a myopic view, having forgotten the truth of my essential divine nature. The need for
walls is an illusion. When you are All, there is no-thing to keep
out. When you are Love, there is no fear, for there is no greater
force in creation.*

Welcome fear, to the warmth of Love's wholeness.

The perspective you hold has moved beyond the limitations
of fear. When you are aligned with your highest essence, you
hold the fine space of Love's light. Within a chaotic expression
of transformation on the planet Earth, your environment may at
times trigger the reflex of fear.

From your space of wholeness, rather than raise the sword of
fear's battle cry, welcome fear home.

The Council of Light

DAY 360: LIVING IN HARMONY

Within *In Service to Love* we have identified ways of being that are integral to your process of aligning with your I AM Self. When you are within the immaculate Now moment, informed by your highest expression, you engage the experience of harmony. When the life you project into the world through your words, actions and thoughts aligns with your inner truth, you experience a flow of being because there is no resistance. Harmony is not an external expression. Harmony reflects an inner alignment.

In the absence of interference, or conflicting expressions, there is just you. All of you present in the Now immaculate moment, with no resistance. Like the ocean's waves, unhindered by the walls of a pool, your expression flows in the most dynamic, potent, and natural way. The magnificence of you may be felt. Your sense of freedom and joy soars, as you BE.

In your alignment, your soul has space for expression. The limited view you have held of yourself is not large enough for your wholeness. It is in aligning your human nature with your divine nature that you access your dynamic, full-on expression.

You know how to do this. Your inner alignment allows space for your ultimate expression to move into form. The potent creative power that is yours requires a large canvas to work upon. Move gently into your space of alignment. Claim your totality powerfully as you run free.

You are the only you there is. One of a kind. Only you may contribute what is yours to share.

DAY 361: THE DEFAULT OF CHOICE

W hen we began our divine collaboration almost a year ago, you held mechanisms in place that delineated your thoughts and behavior, and defined what was possible within your life. The myriad of default mechanisms you have held represented your baseline way of being. The restrictions lived just beneath your conscious awareness and represented a reliable backdrop to your life. Now you have access to the most potent, dynamic Source that informs your life's moments. Now you have access to YOU.

The act of being unconscious searches externally for information, affirmation, and value. Now, as you live within the miraculous environment of the Now immaculate moment, your capacity to reach into the depths of your divine truth is so vast, it is immeasurable. You hold an infinite treasure trove of light, wisdom, Love, and inspiration, to create whatever you choose.

Now your default mechanism truly is choice. Now, as you choose, you reach beyond the limitations of cultural, familial, and environmental thought. You hold the capacity to reach into the still space of your I AM presence and retrieve the divine inspiration that is and always has been yours. You dance the ladder of frequency with an adept quality, on purpose.

And now, your greatest joys and your greatest expression are available in this moment. And Now, your greatest creations and works are possible. All that is yours to be, do, and have is available within the field of possibility that is you.

And Now, all it takes is your choice. Where do you focus your brilliance Now?

Day 362: The Next Expression Calling You Forth

As you move on the gradient scale of light expression that is your totality, your I AM Self continues to ever so gently call you forth into your highest expression. This is not outside you. Enlightenment is a natural manifestation of evolution that continues to invite your awareness into the yet undiscovered realms of your I AM Self.

Your baseline frequency continues to increase as you lean into the realm of the unknown and allow your divine truth to arise in your awareness. The light you access is reflected in your creations as they align more clearly with your truth. Increasingly, you are calling forth that which is yours to BE, DO, and HAVE.

We would like to acknowledge the courage it has taken for you to step out of the deeply held patterns of unconsciousness to strum the strings of your own soul's ballad. As you continue to move forth in your process of expanding awareness, what is it that calls you Now?

From the potency of this Now immaculate moment, allow your I AM to embrace you in the warmth of your own knowing. Again, you are at a threshold. Beyond this threshold lies your next steps. Created within the Now immaculate moment, you may get a sense of the new venture ahead. When you book a ticket for a cruise you have not been on before, you have the itinerary in hand and await the magic of each moment to unfold in perfection before you. The excitement and anticipation fill your senses with the possibility of the unknown. What is next to be revealed?

You see, the completion of this expression of *In Service to Love* is not the end. The next work is already in the queue. As with all creation, there is a next expression. You never stop evolving. We, as the Masters in light, standing for the expansion of Love's light, never stop. We have heard your call, and you have heard our response. We honor our collaboration, in service to Love.

DAY 363: LOVE'S LIGHT

The light of Love is a potent force. The light you reach at the depths of your essence is the light of Love. You have already noticed an order in your life that is forming. There seems to be more of a rhythm and reason to your life. Rather than disparate moments, you see from a more distant perspective the wisdom that has woven your moments together. Nothing is lost. Each moment is a contribution that you bring to the next.

Love's light is an organizing force. As you continue to align with your divine expression and hear more clearly the voice of your soul, you see how Love continues to bring to your attention what is not in alignment with your truth. Through a resonant knowing, Love releases what is not you to reveal the beauty of your true nature.

Love reveals truth. As an earthquake is a process that releases resistance to movement, Love's light releases what no longer serves you. Love's light releases all that is illusory. The light of Love restores alignment, revealing a space of truth and peace sourced by Love. Love's light constantly aligns perspective toward the true north of your divine being: your I AM Self. The light of Love provides a constant beacon directing you, if you so choose, to your highest perspective.

Love's eternal offering is clarity of vision: "I once was blind, but now I see." A new potent view is available every moment. Each step, guided by your soul, illuminates the next step on your path.

As you move within the space of Love's light, you see the transformation occurring in your life as truth is revealed. You are a potent Master creator who has come onto the planet Earth when the need is the greatest. In every incarnation, you have brought the light of Love and an intention to restore truth as a way to ease the pain of misalignment. When one lives in the darkness of illusion, the connection to light feels all but lost. You have always been a champion of those who do not see. Your being, filled with the light of Love, transforms.

You uphold the vision available within Love's light. It is no longer necessary to twist yourself into a pretzel to fulfill someone else's view of reality. You have always known the truth. Now is the time to live your truth. You are informed by Source. All is well. Allow the light of Love that you are to reveal Love's truth as all is held in wholeness.

DAY 364: FULL CIRCLE

You have come full circle. As one inhalation and exhalation bring you to the next, so too has this year of extraordinary movement in light brought you to another beginning. Poised within a new moment, filled with possibility, you choose what is next. However, you do so with a newfound integration within the vast range of light expression that is you. You hold an awareness that spans your totality, not just one point of expression from which your life is created. You now hold your I AM presence as the touchstone for everything.

A new beginning, and you have never been here before. You hold the vast storehouse of wisdom of your essential nature. As with every grand journey, only the next steps are illuminated with the promise of what is yet to come.

We stand beside you in this most potent moment of alchemical transformation. If you so choose, we offer an initiation to close this chapter and to step over the threshold of what is next. You don't need to know what is next. Allow the what is next to arise in your awareness. In this completing process, all that is yours to have, know, and be within our collaboration will be sealed. This is a process that seals the awareness you have gained, and the light you have accessed, into your conscious knowing so you may access it as the broader resource that has always been available yet not opened previously. Now what has been gained will not be illusory. The impact of your divine truth may become an operative focal point of your creative process, if you so choose. This facilitates your moving forward in your life in the most potent, clear, and aligned way. As though in the past you were creating in your life blindly, like an artist before the canvas wearing a blindfold. Now, as your gains in light are sealed, you become consciously aware of your divine, vast perspective with each step, and you create with clarity and vision.

Full-Circle Completion Stargate

This process of full-circle completion is served through the opportunity to avail yourself of a Stargate opening, specifically for this purpose. This Stargate offers three functions:

STEP ONE: Release
Release all that is no longer serving your highest expression. All the ways of being that were habit or unconscious or default are no longer valuable moving forward. Consider releasing all the thoughts, agreements, and restrictions you have held over lifetimes that kept your truth contained. It is time, my Beloveds, to bloom into the divine perfection that is yours.

You do not need to think of everything you have gained. Hold the space of your own wholeness now in comparison with where you were when you began this work. You will feel an automatic release of what no longer serves you. BE with the releasing until you feel it is complete before moving to step two.

STEP TWO: Gather
Gather unto yourself all the movement in light you have gained. Allow the broad perspective of your divine knowing to guide your moments with new clarity and vision. As this new, more clearly aligned way of being becomes the platform for your moments, your creations sing in harmony with the expression of your soul. You walk the steps of the sacred on Earth.

This becomes the new beginning for what is next, after you have released what no longer serves you. This is a space of honor and acknowledgment. Enlightenment is not a passive process. It has taken something for you to BE-come. Now, Beloved, your voice is honored. You are seen. You are met by the divine in light. Each moment becomes the blank canvas upon which you paint your life.

STEP THREE: Declare

When you are ready, declare your movement in light as sealed, and so it is. As you seal your gains in light, you declare that your next steps are grounded in the sacred knowing of your soul.

This Stargate action will be available, closing when you are complete. We suggest you sit down and center yourself. Get clear with each step. The act of releasing, gathering, and sealing in light, forms the new bedrock upon which you build moving forward. The perspectives gained will not be diminished and now become the underlying way of being.

The access to this divine mechanism of the Stargate is available out of who it is that you are. The momentum and in many cases velocity you have created in your expanding awareness, holds potent creative force. You have created this out of your request, intentions, and mission of Love. You have chosen to walk the path of the sacred, expressing all that is yours.

Beloved, we hold you in the divine light of Love's appreciation.

With Love, from Love, for Love,

The Council of Light

DAY 365: AT YOUR FINGERTIPS

At your fingertips you balance the light of your being with manifestation within the physical experience. You are the edge of Love's light that is woven throughout the creation of All. You hold the ability to transform life itself. The extent of your reach into the light of Love allows the brilliance of the sacred to be a voice of consideration.

You, as a Master of light in form, bridge the chasm of dimensional reality, making available the very divine sustenance of being. Each person, in their own beautiful way, awakens in the perfect moment, lending their light to the awakening of the many. It is in the deepest regard we illuminate before you the light that continues to be sustenance for your next steps, as you in turn light the way for those who search for their own sacred expression. You see, what you do for you, you do for All. There is no separation. Your expanding awareness sheds light for All. It must be.

You are held in Grace as you continue the discovery of your divine identity. Your journey expands beyond the barriers of perceived reality into the realms of clear, conscious creation. Your own unique sacred calling is your north star; the clarion call of your I AM.

As we began our divine collaboration, we pointed to the possibility of living life in form beyond the boundaries of physical limitation. Beloved, you are there. You see beyond your perceived limitations. You have touched the holy light of your essence. You hear beyond the physical. You hold the ability to adjust your frequency to find that which you seek. As you step once more into the light of your truth, you unlock the keys to your knowing.

Within the Alliance of Love, we remain in service to Love.

In Love, from Love, with Love,
The Council of Light

Day 366: A New World

The greatest journey one can undertake is the journey to one's own heart. Through the willingness to release the veneer of appearances you access the most profound truth of you.

Beyond an interesting conversation about philosophy, your discovery alters reality. Consider that the reason you came to this work is an extension of your intention for this lifetime; to find your Self. In the process, you release the distraction of the past and the uncertainty of the future to allow yourself to settle into the most potent expression of you, available *only* in the Now immaculate moment. As you consider the possibilities that lie beneath the expected collective template of the best way to live your life, you discover the treasure of your own unique expression as informed by your deepest sacred wisdom.

When you connect with the deep truth of your eternal, sacred nature, you take your place at the table and then live the life that is worthy of you. You look beyond the so-called safety of templates designed by the collective consciousness. Rather than searching within the collective consciousness for your path, you see the brilliance of your truth that may only be viewed from a far broader perspective. You see the collective consciousness as only one arena within which to express. When you first entertain the thought that who you are is Source in form, then, you begin to see beyond the perceived barriers of limited consciousness.

With new vision you are immersed in the magic of the moments of your life. Each moment is a lifetime of exalted beauty. When you BE in alignment with the high frequency of your true eternal nature, not only do you view life differently, you engage the infinite field of possibility with clarity. When the field of possibility is accessed at a high frequency as informed by your I AM presence, your creations in turn hold a high frequency as they are in alignment with your divine nature. Your greatest joy, your greatest freedom, your greatest Love, and everything that is all yours to BE, DO, and HAVE is held in the palm of your hand. All your creations are infused with the divine expressions of Love.

Not only are you transformed in this process, the reality around you is transformed by your presence. When you reach to your I AM as Source for inspiration and guidance, you reach to the purest Source of Love. When Source is the well you rely on for sustenance, everything in your life begins to resonate with the high frequency of your truth. Limitations recede as you touch your infinite expression. Your shift in consciousness changes your reality. Your pure high frequency presence not only resonates with those near you, but your divine light is cast throughout creation, contributing to those you will never see.

Your full presence in the Now moment is the only space that allows you to see clearly the undiluted magnificence of you. With each new discovery into the light expression of your true nature, you bring the brilliant light of your truth into form. You hold a potent creative and expressive stance. In the moment, informed by your highest expression, you create the masterpiece of your soul.

Each and every moment lived allows a new breath of Love's freedom and truth to be reflected through your unique expression. You truly walk upon the earth with sacred footsteps.

Beloved, we remain, In Service to YOU.

In Love, with Love, from Love,

The Council of Light

A Closing from Darlene

The wisdom of our divine nature is available in each moment. Like Dorothy in Oz, we have always possessed everything we need to get home. The process of enlightenment is a rich path for me. It clears a way of being in life so that I can bring my best and live a life that is no longer cluttered with the emotional baggage and energy drain of living life from the outside in. There is no longer a chasm between who I AM and who I BE, as all of me is brought to the exquisite state of beauty and possibility within the Now moment. In an increasingly complicated world, I experience simplicity and the potency that is my soul's voice. Beyond circumstance, I live within the quiet of the eye of the storm.

The process has taken, and continues to require effort as I intend to hold the line between what I know and what I don't know, which opens the door for what is next. There is always the lure of relaxing into the world I now know, because it is comfortable, easier and even ethereal as I reach finer realms of light. We all are at choice in each and every moment. What I have discovered in this process of *In Service to Love* is that who I am is so much larger than the physical life I inhabit. I choose to answer the calling of my soul and step into my greatest role, my wholeness, only revealed in the exquisite beauty of the Now moment.

Thank you for taking this journey. I see you. I recognize you. I honor you as you hold the courage and tenacity to BE Love Now. Together, we stand at another threshold.

In Service to Love,
May 2020
Darlene Green

A Closing from the Council of Light: Sovereignty

After the handrails are gone. After the vows of limitation for this lifetime are dissolved. After you have delved deeply into the unknown of your own soul, sourced by the divine light of Love, you find your sovereignty.

Sovereignty is a state of wholeness where you have access to your essential Self. No longer dependent upon opinions, circumstances, or waiting for a time when it is safe to express all of you, you ultimately find yourself as sovereign, and you realize you have become. You stand in wholeness, radiant, emanating the light of the divine, diminished by no one and no thing. In the peace, magnificence, and stark realization of the moment that you have BECOME, you walk within the light of your wholeness. You experience your divine nature and the beauty of your human nature aligned. Now what becomes possible? In alliance with the divine you walk on Gaia, gathering the universe with the wave of your arm. The potency, the possibility available in the sacred moment! And now what, Beloved? What becomes possible when one IS Love Now?

It is in deep appreciation, honor, and reverence that we, members of the Council of Light, greet you as you take your place at the table.

We remain,
In Service to Love,
May 2020
The Council of Light

In Service to Love Book 1: Love Remembered
In Service to Love Book 2: Love Elevated
In Service to Love Book 3: Love Now

For more works by Darlene Green in collaboration with
the Council of Light,
you are invited to visit darlenegreenauthor.com.

Made in the USA
Columbia, SC
25 September 2020